CONTAINER ATLAS

A PRACTICAL GUIDE TO CONTAINER ARCHITECTURE

SLAWIK, BERGMANN, BUCHMEIER, TINNEY (Eds.)

gestalten

FOREWORD

Starting with the intention of collecting my own buildings and projects under the title of "*Container*Architecture", the dramatic increase in the number of container buildings worldwide led to the idea of producing an atlas that would present an overview of the state of "*Container* Architecture". With the uninterrupted boom in container projects, interest in this subject and the demand for information regarding aspects of the design and construction of containers has also increased.

As the head of the Experimental Design and Construction department within the Faculty of Architecture and Landscape Sciences at Leibniz University Hanover, I was able to draw on the expertise of my academic and research staff to help with the creation of the first container atlas in the world. For a number of years now, container architecture has been the explicit focus of our research activity. This has been accompanied by student designs and seminars with the deliberate aim of increasing our store of "container knowledge".

I would like to sincerely thank the researchers Julia Bergmann, Matthias Buchmeier, and Sonja Tinney for their enthusiasm and unwavering dedication. Our tutors Anja Iffert and Lisa Lüdke also deserve thanks for their contribution.

We would also like to thank Dutch engineer Douwe de Jong for his guest article, which provides more detailed information on the structural aspects of building using freight containers. Special thanks go to entrepreneur Dr Christian Seidel, architectural sociologist Heino Sandfort, and architect Carsten Wiewiorra for their valuable suggestions regarding the manuscript.

Last but not least, we would like to expressly thank the architects themselves and their photographers for their willingness to allow us to use their material.

We invite you, the reader, to take a trip through the world of alternative, "non-bourgeois" architecture. We hope that the *Container Atlas* will help to increase awareness and understanding of this subject, and that this work will serve as a manual for building using containers for specialists and interested laypeople alike.

Prof Han Slawik
2010

After more than 10 years and several German and English reprints, the still-existing demand for *Container Atlas* was reason enough to update this architectural classic. According to container refurbishment companies, many clients come to them holding the book in their hands. I also have many requests from interested parties worldwide, and almost all of them have the book as a source of inspiration.

Covering a generous timeline across several decades and a multitude of projects, the *Atlas* is fast becoming the history book of container architecture—I hope it continues to encourage building with space modules.

Prof Han Slawik
2020

CONTENTS

THE HISTORY OF THE SHIPPING CONTAINER

While young Malcom McLean sat behind the wheel of his truck at the pier in Hoboken, New Jersey, waiting hours for bales of cotton to be unloaded from his truck, he couldn't possibly have known what an impact the idea he had dreamt about that night would have on the world. Rather, he was bored and frustrated because as the owner of a trucking company, every wasted hour cost him hard cash.

Malcom Purcell McLean was born in North Carolina in 1913 and grew up on a farm during the Great Depression. The hard physical work on the farm made him realize from early on, that he wanted to do something different with his life. With only a high school diploma, he left the farm and started to work at a gas station in a town close by. When a construction manager came in one day looking for a driver with a truck, McLean simply went to the local Ford dealer's, bought a used pick-up for $120 and started working for him. He soon realized that he would be able to make good money with a haulage company and started to set up a fleet of trucks. Back then it was hard to imagine that "McLean Trucking Co." would become the second largest trucking company in the USA with 1770 vehicles and 32 terminals. But on his way to the top, there were a couple of setbacks such as the heavy ice storms in 1936 that caused accidents and the cancellation of orders, thus forcing the successful start-up entrepreneur to get back behind the wheel himself. On the aforementioned tour in the following year, he had a revolutionary idea while he was impatiently waiting for the longshoremen to unload his freight of cotton from the truck onto the ship,

bale by bale, with a hook. How easy would it be if one could only take off the whole truck mounting and then, at the ship-to location, just put it on another truck or freight train?

The idea of transporting goods in containers in order to facilitate the process of loading and unloading wasn't new at that time. Since the beginning of the past century, metal boxes had been used for transportation of goods. On the route between Dover and Calais, vehicle-comprehensive modules were even already in use, but none of these systems had made it out of their niche. McLean was seeking a universal solution. The idea of introducing standardized containers the size of a truck's loading space suitable for all major means of transportation was born at that moment, but the path to implementing this system was very long and difficult. None of the sectors whose participation would have been required for the inter-modal container's success were willing to venture out on this new trail. The traditional shipping industry, in particular, was reluctant to accept the bare sheet metal box. Apart from the fact that they did not believe in the concept of mechanically unloading goods, a system such as the one proposed would completely turn existing logistics upside-down. The handling of individually packaged goods was very lucrative for shipping companies because the transport price was composed of many different parameters such as quantity, size, weight and value as well as fees for special handling. Basically, contractors did not have any price transparency or alternatives for sending their goods. And here was this Malcom McLean telling them that with his new system, ships wouldn't have to stay

in harbors any longer than a couple of hours because machines were going to do the unloading. Instead of 20 longshoremen, only one would be needed. Transportation prices would become fairer and more transparent; freight would be handled in bundles and in closed boxes so that the chances of losing goods or having them stolen would be minimized. This whole new way of handling goods would lead to a loss of jobs as well as the cherished harbor romanticism that had a great appeal to many workers in the shipping industry. It would mean the end of extensive shore leaves and the vivid quayside bar culture; no more chances to secretly pocket a carton of cigarettes, a tin of coffee or a few oranges. It was unimaginable that a country boy wanted to eliminate all that.

Like any revolutionary idea that is born, its realization couldn't be stopped. At best, the process could be slowed down—in the case of the shipping container, it took about 20 years. First of all, McLean had to rescue his trucking company. He took his sister Clara and his brother Jim on board and started building terminals throughout the country. Every employee he hired had to begin by going on the road for half a year, because McLean was convinced that only those who had driven themselves and thus had learned how to handle freight, change oil, and maintain the engine were really able to evaluate freight prices. He kept developing new training programs because he regarded well-trained employees as the key to a successful business. Part of his philosophy was the rule that no one was allowed to give trucks names or place nametags inside the driver's cab. This was because he didn't want his drivers to become attached to a particular vehicle as they would then give "their" truck special treatment and wouldn't want to drive other trucks of the fleet. He believed that a company that allowed its employees to develop a personal relationship to one particular truck couldn't run efficiently. Thus, instead of having names, every vehicle at McLean Trucking was starkly numbered. Whenever Malcom McLean launched into something, sensitivities had to yield to profitability.

In 1965, McLean had enough money to make his dream of a universal freight container for ships, trucks and trains come true. Since he still couldn't expect any support from the various transport branches, he decided to become a shipping company owner himself. He bought the Pan-Atlantic Steamship Corporation after fighting stubbornly, and eventually successfully, for a loan that actually exceeded the bank's limit. His competitors were incensed: they sued him, citing the then valid anti-monopoly law, which prohibited companies from operating sea and land transport at the same time. McLean had to choose between his new shipping company and his very successful trucking business, which he had established in tedious work over so many years. Without hesitation, he gave up trucking because he was so obsessed with his new business plan and convinced of its success. When the first container ship, the "Ideal X", with on-board loading bridges, left the harbor of Newark, New Jersey that same year, experts were certain that this was nothing but some very expensive pipe dream that was not going to survive the reality check. His own crew had difficulties with the innovations in their traditional métier, too. When their boss suggested abolishing the ships' names and giving them numbers just as he had done with the trucks, there was almost mutiny. But it was this very novel approach that made him the revolutionary he was. What distinguished him from other ship owners, who mainly thought about shipping, or the truck business owners, who only thought about trucking, was that he was concerned about nothing but the freight. When he opted for the shipping branch and against trucking, he didn't switch to a different industry; he only changed the means of transportation for his freight.

In 1960, the Pan-Atlantic Steamship Corporation was renamed Sealand Services. The new, simple and more direct name mirrored McLean's philosophy that had no room for maritime nostalgia; this company was all about efficiency and success. McLean didn't bother to build new ships—similarly to his former trucking business, he used cargo ships and converted them to hold containers because it saved time and money. The beginnings of Sealand Services were rough: the enterprise had to circumnavigate bankruptcy several times, but all the young employees that

McLean had wisely selected with the help of his siblings were highly motivated and worked hard and enthusiastically for the new idea. Within the following years, more and more container ships landed in US American harbors. While followers commuted between the West Coast and Hawaii, Sealand Services covered the routes along the East Coast. Nevertheless, the old established shipping companies still did not believe in his long-term success, especially in international overseas traffic. When McLean announced that soon he was going to send extremely fast container ships across the Atlantic at intervals of only two days, nobody took him seriously.

Many people are still not quite aware of the great extent to which the freight container influences our life today, even though it has changed consumer behavior dramatically in most parts of the world. Sand shrimp from the North Sea is only available at discount prices in German supermarkets because McLean's containers ship them from Bremen to Mexico and back at a very low cost so that Mexican workers who have probably never tasted sand shrimp in their lives can shell them for a fraction of the wage that a German worker would cost. Today, hardly any final product is assembled in one place anymore; every single component of a thermos flask is produced and added at a different manufacturing plant somewhere in the world. Nations in the most remote corners of the globe now have the opportunity to participate in the world market because no route of transport is as cheap as the one by sea. The introduction of the shipping container has turned oceans into maritime highways.

Back then, the world wasn't waiting for McLean's invention He had to make himself and his ideas known, and the clever businessman sniffed out his great chance during the Vietnam War. Shortly after its outbreak, the US Army experienced difficulty in getting supplies to its soldiers; freight ships loaded with food and military equipment were jammed up outside the harbor of Hanoi because it took so long to unload. With his container system, McLean had the perfect solution for the problem but when he wanted to present it, he wasn't even given an appointment at the Pentagon. Without further ado, he traveled to Arlington, Virginia himself and waited in front of the supply officer's door in order to intercept him on the way to work at seven o'clock in the morning. One last time, his revolutionary idea was greeted with nothing but skepticism. How could this man claim to unload his ships within only 24 hours when everyone else needed at least several days? A free tour arranged right on the spot finally convinced the US government, and a few years later, the rest of the world followed suit. Since the government paid for both ways, back and forth, and McLean didn't want to waste a single traveled sea mile,

he soon started organizing the transport of goods from Japan, Hong Kong and Taiwan for the return trip, thereby causing not only an invasion of Asian foods, toys and electronic devices to the US, but also laying the foundation for globalization.

Finally, the farm boy from North Carolina had won the long battle against the shipping industry and at the same time, eliminated almost all manpower from the process of bringing goods to the people. The few dockworkers left in the harbors have no idea what commodities they are loading and unloading every day at their computer-operated terminals, with the help of driverless vehicles. There is almost nothing that cannot be shipped in a standardized metal box.

INTRODUCTION

FROM THE CONTAINER TO AN ARCHITECTURE

The freight container as a storage and transport vessel for goods revolutionized the transport sector in the last century. Instead of loading and unloading using port cranes or ship cranes, modern global transport is now based on container ships and container terminals. Freight containers can be found all over the world—from the Antarctic to the tropical rain forest.

The "container revolution" began in the 20th century. Malcolm McLean, a former trucking entrepreneur, was one of the first to implement the idea of standardized containers and developed these in 1956 for his trucking empire in the USA in the form of 35-foot-long boxes that could be loaded onto ships. At around the same time, the military was also instrumental in promoting the spread of containers. Back as early as the Second World War, the US Army had already employed rectangular containers as a solution to major logistical problems in crisis areas. The US Army also developed 20-foot boxes that could be transported by water and by land. These developments were then adopted worldwide in the 1960s. Standardization of freight containers in the 1970s, in line with the ISO (International Standards Organization) standard, helped put in place the prerequisites for the worldwide dominance of containers.

The main technical details regarding containers were specified in this ISO standard. The maximum dimensions of containers are mainly determined by the transport conditions, as the locally applicable road traffic regulations prescribe the maximum size of container trailer chassis. 20-foot (6 meters nominal size) and 40-foot (12 meters nominal size) freight containers have become established today from among the various different lengths of container types available. They have a standard width of 8 feet (≈2.4 meters) and various heights: standard cube with 8.5 feet (≈2.6 meters), low cube (rare) with 8 feet (≈2.4 meters) and (increasingly) high cube with 9.5 feet (≈2.9 meters). Transportation and lifting equipment the world over, is tailored to match these dimensions. One 40-foot container or two 20-foot containers can be transported on a single chassis. Alongside the standard containers with lengths of 20 feet and 40 feet, there are also variants and special designs for various purposes: ventilated, cooling, open-top, open-side, bulk, tank, and platform/flat containers.

A standard container consists of a steel construction with standardized special profiles and load-bearing walls. These steel containers are generally made of slow-rusting COR-TEN steel. However, there are also other variants—for example: containers with non-load-bearing wooden wall fillings (plywood containers), those made of aluminum (half the weight, double the price), or containers made of plastics that have a supporting steel frame. The latter, however, have not prevailed.

The load-bearing capacity of containers is also specified in the standard. The containers must be able to withstand deformations in line with specified standard values, and must be fully sealed. Because they are sealed, containers do not sink initially at sea: shipping accidents have resulted in around 30,000 containers currently floating aimlessly on the world's seas—they often lie just under the surface of the water, a potential nightmare for anyone hoping to sail around the world.

001

002

Freight containers are extremely stable: a 20-foot container weighs 2.4 metric tons, can take a load of 24 tons, and can be stacked eight-fold. A 40-foot container weighs 4.5 metric tons, but can only take a load of 30 tons as the load is still only supported by four corners, thus limiting the load-bearing capacity.

Freight containers are also very inexpensive: a new 20-foot container costs around €2,800 and a used one around €1,500. Most containers are produced in Asia and have generally been used once for freight already.

The supporting structure and weather-protective shell is thus available for a price of approximately €200 per square meter or around €75 per cubed meter, a price that is unbeatable when compared to the costs of erecting a conventional building.

Freight containers were first put to new uses in unconverted form. For example, they were used as tool sheds or storage space. The next step was to use freight containers for other purposes, such as for living in, and to convert them accordingly. The load-bearing capacity of shipping containers is very high, but comprehensive conversion work on the basic structure can impair their static properties. As conversion work can be very cost-intensive, the amount of work carried out is often limited by the amount of finance available. Freight containers are almost always used in architecture for temporary construction purposes. Minimum building physics requirements, mainly relating to heat insulation, can be difficult to achieve with unmodified freight containers, however. Containers are favored in event architecture because of their image.

001 | Freight container system

Building containers have become very widespread in the construction industry and are used mainly in Europe. These are containers with a significantly lighter construction that are used as offices or for commercial or housing purposes. They were originally also produced in ISO dimensions, but later on developed their own sizing systems and were fitted with specific transport features. These containers are familiar as construction-site offices, emergency housing for asylum seekers, accommodation in disaster areas, etc. From a statics point of view, it is possible to stack these containers to create up to three stories. They can be stacked up to four stories in exceptional cases, but reinforced constructions must then be used. More stringent building physics requirements, such as those necessary for permanent constructions, can only be fulfilled with increased labor and costs, meaning that building containers are generally only equipped to a minimum standard. They are placed in rows and stacked, and this is generally done without any regard for architectural form. Some manufacturers do make an effort to give

their products a certain quality level by providing more generous facade solutions and by carefully selecting and processing their surface materials—with a commendable degree of success, too. Since these systems are not compatible with similar products from other manufacturers, we refer to these systems as *closed systems*.

002 | Building container system

With all of the systems described so far, the building containers must be custom-manufactured if they are to be joined to produce larger combined spaces. Since fittings components always contribute to load-bearing too, the limits of what is statically permissible can be quickly exceeded if wall, ceiling or floor fillings are omitted. When a number of modules are arranged in rows or stacked, these components double up and are redundant, as there are always two walls, ceilings or floors beside or on top of each other. In principle, the building containers can be reused after being disassembled, but excessive costs may be involved in adapting them to meet new requirements. The sustainability of this building system is thus limited, as the components may need to be processed and treated before being reused.

The principles behind building containers have been transferred to module frames, which can be manufactured in any size, independently of the ISO dimensions system. The fillings also perform a load-bearing function in this building system. This provided the impetus for Professor Han Slawik to develop his own building module, the container frame, and to propose a systematic separation between the load-bearing frame and non-load-bearing fillings. The container frame was the first system to strictly adhere to the idea of adding non-load-bearing fillings to the supporting frame, thus separating the supporting structure and the fittings. There are similar systems available from various manufacturers, but they rely on the shell construction making a contribution to structural strength. This container frame building module has been further developed over the course of various studies, competitions and patent applications. The non-load-bearing fillings are interchangeable in this system, thus guaranteeing maximum flexibility and variability for these modules. With the thermally separated frames and fittings on the frame level and outer premounted shells as an alternative, the building physics requirements could be optimized to a significant extent. The implementation of this type of "pure" system certainly involves more labor and is more costly, but also has the significant advantage that all components created according to a standard, universal system of dimensions are interchangeable and can be reused. Ideally, the components should be industrially manufactured. In the case of mounting, disassembly and remounting where

003

004

the components are reused directly without any modifications, this type of building system that is *open to the market* can be regarded as highly sustainable. Recycling of material or of products—for example in the case of the construction of a skeleton that has to be removed, prepared, or disposed of—is not necessary here. In addition, a supporting frame system can also accommodate do-it-yourself fittings, as the fittings do not have a load-bearing function, thus giving the project team complete design freedom in this regard.

003 | Module frame system
004 | Container frame system (with thermally separated frame profiles)

Building using containers has by now acquired something of a "cult status". The specific image of containers is often important when they are used in architecture, particularly in the event sector. The globalized container box evokes certain associations: the image of a well-traveled item is automatically linked with the raw atmosphere of a busy port, for example. The more striking the building solutions using (freight) containers, the stronger the associative effect of these buildings appears to be.

Despite their strict layout patterns, modular systems based on containers still offer a wide range of spatial solutions. The prerequisite for

this is the positioning of the container—an originally very mobile and extremely unaesthetic box that is available everywhere and is always on the move; a quiet life at a fixed location is not something generally granted to a container. However, this does indeed happen when containers are used in architecture, but the container nonetheless remains mobile and transportable to a limited extent because it can be disassembled.

Building using containers thus often involves more than simply stacking and arranging containers in rows. An architectural structure can only be said to exist if:
- The mobile containers have a fixed location.
- Rooms and spatial connections/openings are created by architectural means, resulting in indoor rooms, intermediate areas, and outdoor spaces.

Only when containers are placed in a spatial context with spatial and architectural qualities do container boxes actually become *container architecture*.

03

USE OF CONTAINERS

Containers are always suitable for use where spatial solutions have to be found for a limited period of time. Container architecture is thus generally found in temporary buildings, where the advantages of a flexible, mobile building system come to the fore. The quick, short-term availability of containers make them effective as building modules. Unfortunately, minimal importance is often attached to architectural quality in the case of temporary building solutions. The frequent repetition of the same building blocks leads to the risk of architectural monotony and anonymity and urban-planning aspects are often ignored too. Construction based on containers used to have a negative image in the past, as a temporary requirement for space is often associated with circumstances where provisional interim solutions are required for people in emergency situations. This effect was often compounded by poor maintenance. However, current examples of container architecture show that solutions that fulfill high architectural standards are indeed possible using containers.

The use of containers in architecture is strongly influenced by the planned usage and the desired effect/impression. The usage strongly affects the type of solution implemented and thus the architectural design too, and low costs also play an important role. The planned service life, which is of course closely related to the usage, is another critical factor. The container is then no longer a mass product when used as a building module, but instead appears as something individual, unique and unmistakable.

The examples of container architecture allow for a categorization according to usage that emphasizes the profile and range of uses for containers in architecture. One can classify projects into public buildings, office buildings, and temporary housing and extensions to housing. Usage as permanent living space is financially most viable in locations where a mild, dry climate is present and protection against heat losses and moisture is not so important. For buildings that meet short-term spatial requirements in a functional manner, architectural design plays a less important role in the selection of the building module. The associated effect, that is attached to freight containers in particular, is used to help generate an image in the commercial sector, for events, for installations in public space, and for art projects involving containers: the image of the container then becomes associated with the product or event too, a process referred to as corporate architecture. Social projects also take advantage of the low acquisition costs of containers (low-budget or no-budget architecture).

A special form of container architecture involves recreated containers that are built using conventional construction techniques, but have the esthetic and structural characteristics of a building container or building container system—the so-called container-look. These are architectural quotes from a construction style that merely suggests a temporary character. In fact, this form of "imitation container" is less efficient from an economic and civil engineering point of view as the advantages associated with prefabrication are lost.

Public buildings

flyport is a passenger terminal that can be implemented anywhere in the world. It has a very short construction time, allows for flexible usage and design, and can be adapted to meet individual needs.

005 | flyport/wolfgang latzel
architekten, 2004: Public buildings

Office

The headquarters of the PLATOON agency, a creative collective active in the area of communications, is located on an undeveloped site right in the middle of Berlin's lively Mitte district. The building consists of an ensemble of freight containers in military green, together with a lawn area and a pool.

006 | PLATOON headquarters/PLATOON,
2007: Office

Housing

This home in California uses freight containers as additional room modules. Used freight containers are freely available and thus also inexpensive in the USA because of the skewed balance of trade where imports exceed exports (Redondo Beach House/DeMaria Design).

007 | Redondo Beach House/
DeMaria Design, 2008: Housing

Social/low budget architecture

Containers are suitable for use in charitable organizations funded by donations such as Children's Activity Centre (Phooey Architecture) in Melbourne, a social facility for children that doesn't charge for admission and therefore has to survive on public subventions.

008 | Children's Activity Centre/Phooey
Architecture, 2007: Social low-budget
project

Commercial/corporate architecture

The mobile PUMA salesroom by the architects LOT-EK consists of 24 shipping containers staggered to form a three-story sculpture. The product being sold, sports and leisure footwear will of course already have traveled the globe in just such a container. The associative interplay of product and architecture results in "corporate architecture".

009 | PUMA/LOT-EK, 2006: Corporate
architecture

Event/exhibition

The Nomadic Museum (Shigeru Ban) employs containers in two ways: as building blocks that form the supporting structure for this large-scale exhibition hall, and as transport containers for building elements and for the exhibition display specimens themselves. Additional containers can also be rented locally, as required.

010 | Nomadic Museum/Shigeru Ban, 2005:
Exhibition

The Illy Café (Adam Kalkin) was developed for a temporary use with a predefined duration as part of the 52th Biennale in 2007 in Venice. At the push of a button, a container that appears unmodified from the outside folds out into a café platform, thus becoming an exhibition object itself.

011 | Push Button House — Illy Café/
Adam Kalkin, 2005: Event

Art

The Belgian architect and artist Luc Deleu uses freight containers in his art by stacking them to create monumental structures and landmarks that can be seen from far around. The containers used are often exaggerated in an artificial manner because of the way they are stacked without their essential forms being changed.

012 | Middelheim Construction X/
Luc Deleu, 2003: Art

Container look

The projects in the "Container look" category are built in a conventional way, but are intended to resemble containers. These buildings merely refer to the esthetic and structural features of containers or container systems, and actually have little in common with container architecture.

They are often structural elements of secondary importance, such as additions to roofs or extensions (parasite architecture). The addition of these "pseudo-containers" is often a deliberate attempt to suggest a process of subsequent, often temporary extensions to a building, even when these secondary components were actually built at the same time as the main building structure itself.

013 | Sjakket Youth Center/
PLOT = JDS + BIG, 2007: Container look
014 | Wismar Technology and Business
Center/Jean Nouvel with Zibell+Partner,
2003: Container look

The use of imitation containers is somewhat odd from an architectural point of view, and this approach is also less than favorable from a civil engineering point of view since the imitation of prefabrication using conventional construction methods is actually very inefficient.

Nonetheless, an imitation container can help to liven up the architectural impression made by a building.

It is possible that container-like spatial cells are recreated for practical reasons in a certain context instead of using ready-made containers (for example: the facade openings might be too small to allow containers to be transported into the building). One possible alternative here would be to use special constructions that can be collapsed (e.g. folding containers).

Certain buildings appear similar to container architecture based on their architectural structure, but these are often simply skeleton structures that follow a strict modular layout. The appearance of a building constructed from spatial cells is created by borrowing the proportions of containers for the pattern dimensions and by repeating identical openings at regular intervals.

015 | Distributiecentrum Piet Zoomers/
Van den Belt & Partners, 1992: Container
look
016 | Student housing/Mecanoo
Architekten, 2009: Container look

005

006

007

008

009

010

011

012

013

014

015

016

04

CONTAINERS AS BUILDING MODULES

017

DEFINITION

Containers were originally conceived as vessels for goods, but are also used as spatial modules in architecture. The word "contain" comes from the Latin "continere", and means to hold together, to surround, to store. A container is a vessel that surrounds a usable volume of space and thus defines the spatial boundary between interior and exterior. As a walk-in box with useful spatial dimensions, the container fulfills the prerequisites for use as a spatial module.

Geometrically, a container is a six-sided rectanguloid with at least one opening. The standardized dimensions generally adhere to the internationally applicable ISO standard for freight containers. This standard has had a long-term influence on container use everywhere and provides the basis for the sizing of containers.

These dimensions are primarily determined by the transport conditions and by the infrastructure present.[1]

The structure of a container is a combination of a frame and fillings. The frame supports the fillings that define the spatial boundaries; these fillings are generally also load-bearing and provide reinforcement for the building. Both static and dynamic loads must be taken into account when using containers. The static loads result from self-weight and the contents, while dynamic loads occur during transportation and mounting.

As a transportation vessel, the container is of course mobile. Transportation is of varying significance, depending on the usage in question. The importance of transportation when a container is used as a building module is different

018

019

020

021

from that when it is employed as a shipping container: while a shipping container fulfills its function by transporting its contents, a building container only serves its actual purpose when it is used as a building.

The container has transport devices at its eight corners that are used to distribute all loads and to combine modules using joining devices to create a supporting system. The containers fit on standardized platforms, such as the chassis of a truck, where they can be fastened for transportation by road, rail or ship. The containers are moved using cranes and other lifting equipment.

PRINCIPLES

Containers are conceived as single-room modules that can form a flexible multi-room system once they are combined. The spatial system adheres to the modular layout system of container modules, which allows for relatively little freedom. Variations are possible within this layout principle, and empty and intermediate rooms can be created by omitting containers. However, it should be taken into account that vertical loads are distributed exclusively through the corners. When modules are combined, horizontal loads are also supported and transmitted by the joint devices.

017 | Containers as a single-room/
flexible multi-room systems (system-
compatible)

Containers are generally positioned horizontally and supported at four points; they are designed for this scenario. Alternatively,

containers can also be placed vertically to serve as symbols or landmarks—this represents a special case in terms of structural design, however. Experimental projects provide examples where containers are positioned vertically and are even designed as spaces with various accessible stories.

018 | Horizontal/vertical positioning

Interior connections between the containers are also horizontal/vertical, as required by the container layout. Because of load-bearing capacity constraints, the number of containers that can be stacked is between three and eight, depending on the construction system in question. To create spatial and functional linkages, appropriate openings are necessary that may be subject to certain constraints, depending on the system.

019 | Horizontal/vertical connection
(longitudinal side)
020 | Horizontal/vertical connections
(short side)

When combining container modules, it should be ensured that loads are supported by the corners, and thus that the corners are positioned above one another in order to transmit the loading to the ground effectively. If this is ensured, one speaks of system-compatible joints. In the case of deviations from this system, such as staggering or rotation of container modules relative to other modules, reinforcements are necessary at those points where corners meet a frame beam. These are then joints that are not system-compatible, which generally also result in a deviation from the standard dimensioning system.

021 | Staggering/rotation of containers
(deviating from system)

When building using room modules, the system of dimensions of the room modules determines the axis grid pattern. Since a tolerance between the containers must also be taken into account, the axis grid length is made up of the container dimension plus the tolerance. This system also holds in the vertical direction. This interrelationship is also part of the dimension system in the ISO standard.

022

023

024

022 | Dimensional interrelationships
when joining containers (axis grid =
container dimension + tolerance)

In principle, containers can be joined to create self-supporting buildings where the containers act as the room-defining elements. However, it is also possible to use containers solely as a supporting structure, to stack them to form wall structures, and to create intermediate spaces using for example, a secondary roof-supporting structure that rests on wall structures made of containers. The structural strength of the container type is of critical importance here. Non-load-bearing containers can also be slid into a primary supporting structure and can thus define rooms without directly supporting loads from the rest of the building. This system provides maximum flexibility with regard to interchangeability and extensions for applications where connections between the various rooms are not of primary importance.

023 | Containers as a supporting struc-
ture/non-load-bearing containers

In the case of simple container building systems, every individual module has its own structural weather and climate shell. As container systems have certain structural engineering weaknesses, it may be a good idea to place the

containers under a protective roof in order to avoid problems caused by leaks in the roof cladding, for example. The most radical solution is to place the containers inside an additional shell that fulfills a weather-protection and insulation function, if necessary.

024 | Containers with weather/climate
shell and protective roof

FOUNDATION

Container buildings always require a foundation in addition to their overground structures. The type of foundation to be used depends on the geometry and more importantly, on the planned service life of the building. In the case of mobile buildings, foundation types that are demountable and leave no traces are to be preferred ahead of foundations made from site-mixed concrete.

Foundations that use large prefabricated concrete slabs (such as those made by Stelcon) are suitable as they can be installed easily and quickly. They are available in standard sizes between 2×1 meters and 2×2 meters. The slab thickness is around 14cm. The subsurface must be prepared accordingly before installation is carried out. The slabs are placed on a mineral mixture and a sand layer of coarse and fine sand that compensates for unevenness of the ground.

025 | Slab foundation (e.g. Stelcon)

Alternatively, there are single foundations or screw foundations that are screwed into the ground using a motor or a similar boring machine. These can be easily removed in the same way, leaving behind no traces, and are thus even reusable. Some foundation types are compressed with granulate.

026 | Screw foundation

Prefabricated pad foundations made of precast concrete parts (pin foundation, removable pre-cast concrete foundation) are also suitable as foundations. A precast concrete part is fixed in the ground here using steel rods sunk into the ground at an angle.

027 | Pin foundation

In general, the container must be fixed to the ground at its four corners using adjustable steel footings whose height can be evened out; these footings transfer loads to the ground. The fastening holds the building in place and also protects it from being lifted up by wind loads.

Since container buildings are very light, it may be necessary to provide a counterweight in the foundation area or to use weights to load down certain parts of the building—for example in the case of very high buildings. Solid, site-mixed concrete foundations can be used here, but for more temporary usages it is a

025

026

027

better idea to fill containers with sand or to use water tanks.

Floating constructions can also be implemented using containers. In this case, installation is either carried out on standard floating pontoons or on <u>container pontoons</u> that already have standard container dimensions (20 feet or 40 feet) and can be joined together. They are equipped with suitable corner brackets. The height of the pontoons is either the same as, one half of, or one third of the usual height of a standard container.

CONSTRUCTION PHYSICS

As a rule, civil engineering weaknesses in the structure of containers only allow for temporary usage. Containers can generally be classified as light building modules, which also has an effect on thermal insulation in summer and winter. The absence of solid matter means that container buildings have a <u>low heat capacity</u>. A change in the outdoor temperature thus leads to excessive cooling off or to overheating more quickly than would be the case with a solid structure.

Depending on the system, spatial modules are either insulated during production (building containers, module frames) or else have to be fitted with insulation later on (freight containers). They can then theoretically be equipped to meet almost any <u>thermal insulation standard</u>, but it should be remembered that large material thicknesses for interior insulation also result in a corresponding loss of indoor space. In addition, containers also have thermal bridges inherent in their design at their corners.

Conventional insulating materials are generally used. If there are higher requirements for thermal insulation in winter, or if it is important to make maximum use of the indoor space available, it can be a good idea to use <u>vacuum insulation</u>. This is more laborious to install, is more expensive and does not last as long (maximum manufacturers' warranties of 20 years) but has much better performance than stan 350 °C). Additional measures are thus required in order to meet fire protection requirements. For

example, the fire resistance of components can be increased by adding gypsum plasterboards or plaster coatings that foam up if a fire occurs (F30—F90). Depending on the fire resistance of the structure, there may be approval limits with regard to multi-story designs.

CONSTRUCTION LAW

Construction law differs from country to country and state to state, meaning that it is difficult to make universally applicable statements regarding legal construction requirements. Further information about legal building regulations should be obtained from the relevant local authorities.

The status of temporary container constructions regarding building and finance law can be difficult to define. Container facilities are considered to be temporary[2] in Germany if they are installed for a very short period of time. This applies to construction-site containers for example, which are not classified as buildings; there is no need to apply for planning permission for these structures.[3] In all other cases, container buildings are subject to the same permission requirements as conventional buildings and <u>do not have a special status</u>. The applicable heat insulation ordinance must be adhered to in order to obtain permanent building approval (installation for longer than three years). A lower thermal insulation standard can be accepted for limited-period building approval.

ECONOMIC ASPECTS

Container facilities are generally erected with a significantly shorter construction period than would be necessary for conventional buildings. <u>Short planning and implementation periods</u> can reduce investment costs, and this advantage may tip the balance in favor of a container building.

Depending on the standard of fittings to be used, lower construction costs may also apply: industrial processes can produce container buildings more cheaply than would be the case with conventional construction methods. The costs should be considered relative to the planned service life of the structure. However, it should also be remembered here that additional costs for transportation, foundations and connections to utilities will arise. Regarding transportation, it should be taken into account that the world-wide shipping of a freight container is relatively inexpensive[4], even over great distances; however, the transportation of a building container by truck can be considerably more costly.[5] In particular, the transportation of special loads by road is laborious and expensive.

Prices for raw materials such as steel fluctuate strongly depending on demand on the world market. Possible future uses, resale of the modules after the planned service life, and disposal all influence the costs later on.

The required standard of fittings for the building plays an important role in the decision in favor of or against a container building, as it may only be possible to meet demanding civil engineering requirements in terms of insulation, fire protection, noise transmittal and other safety requirements to a limited degree. These issues should be examined for each project and the costs should be compared with the investment costs for a permanent structure.

Tax issues may also favor the use of container buildings. However, care should be exercised here: a structure made from containers is not necessarily allowed to be depreciated over a shorter period in Germany. This only applies to buildings that actually have a very short use period. The critical issue here is the degree to which a building is tied to its location. Evaluation of this criterion is independent of the potential mobility that is always inherent in container buildings. A container structure can be categorized as having a fixed location if a foundation base exists (which need not necessarily be permanently installed). Use as a permanent residence, the existence of sanitary facilities or connections to the public supply grid can all make a container building an integral part of the site from a legal evaluation point of view. Container buildings that are adjudged to be tied to their locations are classified as light buildings, and these can then be depreciated over a shorter period of time than solid-construction buildings.[6] Modular construction generally results in fixed-location buildings. Tax law treats these buildings in the same way as conventional buildings.

The decision whether to rent or buy the containers should always be based on the planned service life of the building and on any conversion work that may be necessary. Buying is generally a better option for usage periodslonger than 24–36 months. The price for purchasing a new container module varies depending on the system, and used containers can also be bought as an alternative for around 50% of the new price.

ECOLOGICAL ASPECTS

Container architecture has significant advantages compared to conventional construction methods from an environmental point of view. As container building blocks are inherently demountable and remountable, it is possible to reuse the modules once the planned service life of the building is over. The building can be disassembled into individual, stand-alone spatial units. Modularity also means that the system can be extended.

Because of the short time it takes to erect a container building, it is possible to react more quickly and flexibly to increasing spatial requirements and to planning changes by gradually extending the structure. In addition, gradual building extensions are also possible. For example, a smaller part of a commercial building can be built initially for a company start-up, and the building then completed later on when extensions become necessary. In this way, unoccupied building space can be avoided.

The period of use of the container should be carefully considered. In principle, the expected service life of the basic frame structure (supporting construction) is longer than that of the fittings and finishing. The building services technology in particular, quickly becomes obsolete after a few years (technical equipment). The container is then disposed of after its full service life is over. The steel can be reused as a raw material, as it can be better recycled than concrete for example, which can only be reprocessed for lower-grade uses. The investor can even recoup a small portion of the investment costs by selling the recycled steel; other construction waste has to be disposed of at a cost, however. Depending on the particular design, a container can contain between 0.5 and 4.0 metric tons of steel, which can be sold at the scrap price[7] that is currently applicable. In the case of rental, the owner has to bear the disposal costs.

In addition, it is also possible to supply container buildings using alternative energy sources. For example, it is possible to integrate solar panels or photovoltaic equipment into the outer shell or the roof. These generate energy and also help to reduce problems with excessive temperatures inside the container building in summer by providing shading.

INTERNATIONAL ASPECTS

When comparing the international situation, it can be observed that containers are available and used as building modules the world over. However, it can be assumed that the type and frequency of use, the selection of container type, and the intended purpose are all strongly dependent on certain local considerations:

1) Climate: The requirements placed on the quality of the climate shell are as varied as the climates themselves. The heat insulation

requirements are legally stipulated in some countries, while this is not the case in other regions. Because of the mild climate conditions in California for example, there are many residential projects based on shipping containers there that only have to fulfill modest requirements in terms of thermal insulation.

2) Distance: Long transportation distances and high costs for transportation will apply for regions with lower population densities. For this reason, the transportability of the building can be of much greater significance here as compared to other regions. One of the reasons the "trailer" model is common in the United States is probably because it is already fitted with a chassis and can thus be transported more easily and cheaply.

3) Cultural influences: Cultural norms can also play a role in the decision for or against a temporary (container) building. Mobility is an integral part of people's living habits in the USA, for example. When moving home in rural areas, it is sometimes even possible to take advantage of light modular constructions and effectively take your house with you. In Germany, buying real estate and private homes is still seen as a long-term investment, meaning that more solid constructions tend to be favored. The image associated with container buildings varies too from region to region: although a lot of construction is taking place in China, container buildings are not widespread because container units with trapezoidal sheeting are regarded as inferior.

4) Global economic influences: Economic conditions can also influence the use of containers; in particular, the type and amount of trade (import/export) plays an important role here. For example, a lot more goods are imported into the USA in shipping containers than are exported out of the country, meaning that there is an excess of containers at American container terminals. Thus, they are sold relatively cheaply. In 2008, the financial crisis had also led to an excess of freight containers worldwide simply because less goods are being transported than before. The currently falling prices for steel are also reducing prices and production costs for containers.

5) Regional economic circumstances: Cost-effective building can be a significant factor in economically less-developed regions. Commercial and educational buildings and infrastructural facilities such as airports can be built for low investment costs in order to stimulate the economic development of certain regions. In addition, a building system that can be erected at short notice can generally react a lot quicker to changing economic circumstances.

6) Structural statics requirements: The requirements for structural stability can also vary depending on the region in question. Steel constructions are particularly suitable in areas with a risk of earthquakes such as Japan, as they exhibit elastic behavior when subject to vibrations.

05

CONTAINERS AS BUILDING BLOCKS

Containers are universally applicable building modules in the construction sector. They are available in various types and for various purposes. The range of uses is just as wide: from functional buildings right through to experimental, architecturally demanding custom solutions.

The following categorization forms the basis for the design consideration of container architecture—containers will be considered under the headings: freight containers, building containers and module frames/container frames.

028

TYPE 1
FREIGHT CONTAINERS

028 | Isometric drawing of a freight
container

029

030

For a number of years now, freight containers have been subject to reappropriations in terms of their function and have been finding increasing use in architecture. There are two main aspects that make containers attractive in architectural applications: their characteristic design that can be used to create a certain image, and their system-based advantages such as prefabrication, modularity, global availability, and low unit prices.

However, these benefits must be weighed up against certain civil engineering disadvantages too. Containers are accessible when loading and unloading their contents, and offer a sealed shell and a certain minimum amount of weather-protection depending on the goods being transported; however, they cannot fulfill important civil engineering requirements for a building shell such as provision of daylight and protection against heat, moisture, noise and fire unless certain conversion and extension measures are carried out.

The space inside a container is only suitable for human occupation to a certain extent because of the limited height on offer. The height is sufficient to be able to stand or walk upright, but more comfortable room heights, which may also be stipulated by construction regulations, can only be achieved with high cube containers.

Nonetheless, the appropriate use of freight containers in construction can lead to quite remarkable architectural solutions. These are characterized by an intelligent architectural treatment of the properties and features of containers. There are three main strategies that can be taken:

Acceptance: The freight container is used in its original form, and the existing finishing and product characteristics are accepted as part of the architectural design. The usage concept is focused on the container not as a place where people will spend a lot of time, but rather as a pre-defined room with a correspondingly low standard in terms of fittings and equipment. In certain cases, it may not even be possible to enter the container, which is instead used as a supporting structure, has advertising mounted on it, or is itself part of an artwork.

029 | Speybank/Luc Deleu, Yokohama, Japan, 2005

Fittings and equipment: A freight container is treated as a raw building module that can be fitted with further equipment and features. The container can then be converted and upgraded subsequently to the desired standard with regard to fittings and technical equipment. This type of use can be particularly labor-intensive when constructing residences because of the high standard of fittings required. However, the advantages of a high degree of prefabrication can also be exploited by carrying out the conversion and upgrading work in a workshop.

030 | Campus/Professor Han Slawik, Almere, the Netherlands, 1992

Combination: To bring the fittings standard to an acceptable level, the container is combined with further components that fulfill the requirements of the planned building usage. This could include an external facade or roof construction, or a completely separate climate shell (house inside a house). A cost-effective alternative is the use of containers indoors only—for example, to divide off smaller functional units inside of larger, existing building structures. In this case, no labor-intensive conversion or fittings work on the container is necessary; instead, minimal conversion measures suffice to make the container suitable for use as an occupied space.

DEFINITION

The freight container system cannot be defined solely by the properties of the individual containers. Containers are the core of the system, but only form a transport system when other aspects are considered such as logistics, transport and their ability to be combined.

This is emphasized by the main requirements placed on a uniform transport system, which always has the aim of simplifying and increasing the efficiency of the shipping of goods:
- Uniform transport of differing loads using uniform containers
- Closed transport chains with no reloading of goods along the way
- Reusable containers

The implementation of this sort of transport system called for the specification and standardization of its main elements, and this is exactly what was achieved with the introduction of the ISO standard internationally. This standard is updated at regular intervals and is adjusted for technical and logistical conditions.[8]

STANDARD

The International Standardization Organization (ISO) established a committee with 26 participating countries in 1961 with the goal of standardizing the transport systems that until then, had been very different in Europe and America.

The main aim of the ISO standard that was eventually approved by the 26 participating countries in 1964, was to ensure the functionality and compatibility of the container transport system. For this reason, the standard mainly deals with dimensional, geometrical and use-dependent specifications. On the other hand, the production and structural design of containers remain largely untouched by the standard.

America's influence led to all container dimensions in the ISO standard being specified using the imperial measurement unit of the foot (conversion: 1 foot = 0.30479 meters). This meant that the specification of the interior dimension of the 8-foot-wide ISO container did not allow for loading with two adjacent Euro pallets (80 × 120 centimeters), with the result that the width is a few centimeters too narrow for this purpose.[9]

The core of the container standard is ISO 668, which contains all specifications necessary for the standardization of the container system.

Alongside the definition and classification of standard containers, the standard also deals with all relevant dimensions (internal and external dimensions, door opening dimensions) the construction tolerances for these, and the geometry and positions of the corner fittings for transportation and fastening. Freight containers that are manufactured to meet the specifications of ISO 668 are referred to as ISO containers.

Further standards deal with the terminology of various container types (ISO 830), classification (ISO 6346) and the specification of corner fittings (ISO 1161).

DIMENSIONS

To ensure optimum compatibility, the dimensions of standard containers are modularly structured. The starting module here is the 40-foot (type A) long container, and the other sizes (nominal sizes: 10 feet [type D], 20 feet [type C], 30 feet [type B]) are fractions of this starting length. In order to facilitate stacking and moving of the containers, low tolerances of ¼ inch per 10 feet are taken into account, meaning that a nominal 20-foot container is actually only 19 feet 11½ inches (6,058 mm) long.

The 20-foot container is the most widespread size. It has been adopted for the TEU (twenty-feet equivalent unit) measurement unit that is used in specifying transportation and manufacturing capacities. 20-foot and 40-foot containers have established themselves in shipping and truck transportation because of the ease with which they can be combined.

A standard width of 8 feet has been specified for freight containers to suit the requirements of road transport. Container widths that deviate from this can only be integrated into the ISO system if the positions of the corner fittings remain unchanged.

The standard height (standard cube) is 8 feet 6 inches. In addition, there is the low cube (height 8 feet), and a high cube that was also introduced into the standard in 1992 (height 9 feet 6 inches). The height dimensions are not modular, but are instead based on structural considerations, as the containers can be stacked individually regardless of their height.[10]

Alongside the standardized dimensions specified in the standard, containers with special sizes are also developed every so often, mainly with the goal of maximizing economic efficiency. The main special lengths in use for containers are 45 feet, 48 feet, 49 feet and 53 feet, as these

40' basic dimension

20'/20'

10'/10'/10'/10'

tolerance dimension

10'/30'

032

H

9'6" · 2,896 m (high cube)
8'6" · 2,591 m (standard cube)
8' · 2,438 m (low cube)

10' · 2,991 m (3 m)

20' · 6,058 m (6 m)

W

30' · 9,125 m (9 m)

40' · 12,192 m (12 m)

45' · 13,716 m

8' · 2,438 m

L

033

Desig-nation	Nominal size	Nominal height	External length		External width		External height		Minimum internal dimensions			Door opening dimensions	
									heigth	width	length	height	width
1AAA	40'/12 m	High cube	40'	12,192 mm	8'	2,438 mm	9' 6"	2,896 mm	2,655 mm	2,330 mm	11,998 mm	2,566 mm	2,286 mm
1AA	40'/12 m	Standard cube	40'	12,192 mm	8'	2,438 mm	8' 6"	2,591 mm	2,350 mm	2,330 mm	11,998 mm	2,261 mm	2,286 mm
1A	40'/12 m	Low cube	40'	12,192 mm	8'	2,438 mm	8'	2,438 mm	2,197 mm	2,330 mm	11,998 mm	2,134 mm	2,286 mm
1AX	40'/12 m	—	40'	12,192 mm	8'	2,438 mm	<8'	<2,438 mm	—	2,330 mm	11,998 mm	—	2,286 mm
1BBB	30'/9 m	High cube	29' 11¼"	9,125 mm	8'	2,438 mm	9' 6"	2,896 mm	2,655 mm	2,330 mm	8,931 mm	2,566 mm	2,286 mm
1BB	30'/9 m	Standard cube	29' 11¼"	9,125 mm	8'	2,438 mm	8' 6"	2,591 mm	2,350 mm	2,330 mm	8,931 mm	2,261 mm	2,286 mm
1B	30'/9 m	Low cube	29' 11¼"	9,125 mm	8'	2,438 mm	8'	2,438 mm	2,197 mm	2,330 mm	8,931 mm	2,134 mm	2,286 mm
1BX	30'/9 m	—	29' 11¼"	9,125 mm	8'	2,438 mm	<8'	<2,438 mm	—	2,330 mm	8,931 mm	—	2,286 mm
1CC	20'/6 m	Standard cube	19' 11½"	6,058 mm	8'	2,438 mm	8' 6"	2,591 mm	2,350 mm	2,330 mm	5,867 mm	2,261 mm	2,286 mm
1C	20'/6 m	Low cube	19' 11½"	6,058 mm	8'	2,438 mm	8'	2,438 mm	2,197 mm	2,330 mm	5,867 mm	2,134 mm	2,286 mm
1CX	20'/6 m	—	19' 11½"	6,058 mm	8'	2,438 mm	<8'	<2,438 mm	—	2,330 mm	5,867 mm	—	2,286 mm
1D	10'/3 m	Low cube	9' 9¾"	2,991 mm	8'	2,438 mm	8'	2,438 mm	2,197 mm	2,330 mm	2,802 mm	2,134 mm	2,286 mm
1DX	10'/3 m	—	9' 9¾"	2,991 mm	8'	2,438 mm	<8'	<2,438 mm	—	2,330 mm	2,802 mm	—	2,286 mm

034

45'

40'

037

can be integrated into the existing module system by employing additional corner fittings. A 45-foot container can be transported by road on a standard chassis.

036 | 45-foot containers stacked with
ISO containers
037 | 45-foot container

Completely new length module systems are also being discussed, such as a 49-foot/24-foot module that could replace the existing 40-foot/20-foot module in the long term.

The so-called "pallet wide" containers developed for the efficient loading of Euro pallets are compatible with the ISO standard despite having internal dimensions which are a few centimeters larger, as the frame construction including corners is unchanged even though

the external walls have been shifted relative to the standard container.

The DB inland containers that are solely intended for use by German State Railways on its freight trains are no longer in conformance with ISO with their width of approximately 2.5 meters, but were designed to make optimal use of the rail gauge of the German railway network and are thus an island solution providing the most efficient solution for rail freight.[11]

WEIGHTS AND LOADS

Freight containers are designed to be able to carry heavy loads, and can thus support a multiple of their own self-weight—for example, a 20-foot container can support ten times its own weight. Containers are thus generally considerably oversized for use in architecture.

Container	Self-weight	Loading	Total weight
45'	5,000 kg	25,680 kg	30,480 kg
40'	4,000 kg	26,480 kg	30,480 kg
30'			25,400 kg
20'	2,330 kg	21,670 kg	24,000 kg
10'			10,160 kg

038

standard   hard top   open top   open side

flat   platform   tank

039

Self-weight is an important criterion with regard to the quality of a container. The minimum weight must also be observed, as it reflects the amount of steel used and thus indicates that the necessary static stability has been provided.

038 | Table with self-weights and loadings

The maximum loading of containers is generally not determined by the permitted loading weight but instead by the loading volume, as the permitted total weight is generally only achieved with particularly heavy loads. For this reason, comparatively low loadings are accepted for long containers (40-foot, 45-foot), as the permitted loadings for the corner fittings, which are the same for all containers, must not be exceeded.

TYPES

Based on the standardized dimensions, there is a variety of series container types that are mostly defined by the ISO 830 standard (container vocabulary).

The various types have been developed based on their suitability for the load in question so that different types of goods (piece goods/bulk materials, perishable, heavy, bulky or liquid loads) can be transported in a uniform manner.

039 | Freight container types

A standard container has five closed sides and an opening at one end with a double-leaf door. It is intended for piece goods of all kinds.

040 | Standard containers

The hard top container can be loaded with heavy, bulky goods thanks to its completely removable roof. The container frame is designed to be accordingly stronger.

An open top container is open at the top, but does not have a fixed roof. The cross beams above the doors can be removed to improve loading flexibility. The open roof is generally covered with a plastic sheet.

041 | Stacked, covered open top containers

The longitudinal side of open side containers can be opened completely. The necessary reinforcing bars can be removed to facilitate loading by forklift, for example.

A bulk container has filling openings in the roof and emptying devices that are generally located in the door leaves.

Platforms have a permitted total weight of 34 metric tons and are designed for particularly heavy loads. They consist solely of extremely

040

041

042

043

043

strong base constructions that are higher than those on standard containers. They can be stacked when not loaded, and can be transported on conventional chassis.

Container flats consist of a high-strength floor construction with two foldable end walls. These end walls make it possible to stack a number of loaded flats on top of one another, which is not possible with platforms.

042 | Locking for flats (conical)

A ventilated container, which is aerated through splash-proof ventilation openings in the top and bottom cross beams, was originally specially developed for the transportation of raw coffee, which is the reason why they are also referred to as "coffee containers".[12]

Thermal containers have an insulated outer shell that prevents or at least minimizes temperature fluctuations inside the shell. When fitted with the appropriate equipment, this container can also be used as a refrigerated container (or "reefer container").

A tank container consists of a strengthened and reinforced container frame with an integrated pressure tank where chemicals, fuels or foodstuffs such as fruit juices or liquor can be transported.[13]

In addition to these standardized container types, there are other special designs for specific purposes that could also come into consideration for architectural uses.

For example, there are containers with openings that vary in number, size and position. Containers with doors at both ends are designed so that they can be loaded at both ends, but they could also be glazed at both ends (to provide daylight) as the frame construction allows for this. Containers with openings in the side walls allow for containers to be combined to create larger spatial units.

043 | Containers with side doors and openings for loading

Containers can be equipped with additional fittings to make them suitable for certain types of loads—for example, with textile linings (so-called "liner bags") or other special technical equipment.

COSTS

In principle, two different quality levels can be identified in the international container trade:

Used containers

There are no standard criteria for used containers because of the different uses and loads they may have had. They are thus generally bought only after visual inspection. They are a number of years old, show signs of their age, and may be damaged or dirty.

New container (almost new/as new)

It is almost impossible to buy factory-new

containers in Europe. "New" containers have generally already been used for at least one loaded sea journey from the Far East. However, the value of an individual container does not drop significantly because of this one sea journey. There will generally be little damage or signs of use.

The price of freight containers depends on the (often quite considerable) fluctuations in the price of steel and the exchange rate for the dollar. The price fluctuations are amplified by the purchasing policy of large shipping companies, which directly affects demand, supply and thus also the price. In addition, the costs for storage and logistics for unused containers, which are often considerable, are an important consideration for shipping companies.

Political crises can also influence availability, as the movement of troops and of military equipment also gives rise to enormous transportation requirements.

Another cost factor results from geographical factors relating to goods transport. For example, freight containers are less expensive in regions with an excess of imports (e.g. the west coast of the USA) than in areas where exporting dominates (e.g. Southeast Asia).

The price (including delivery) for a new 20-foot container (TEU) is currently around €2,600—€3,000, and that of a used container is around €1,400–€1,600.[14]

The quality standard of the various shipping companies should be taken into account when buying used containers, as these companies often demand higher manufacturing standards so that they can save on maintenance work later on.

Rental costs for containers (TEU) vary considerably depending on the duration of rental, and delivery costs also play an important role. As a rule of thumb, rental charges of around €120 per month can be assumed, dropping to around €60 per month for longer rental periods. Thus the rental costs exceed the purchasing price after two years at the latest. Considering the residual value too, it is clear that rental is only viable for very short rental periods, as is the case with transport usage. Purchasing is the only realistic option for building applications, especially for conversion projects.

As delivery is a significant contributor to costs, efficient transportation solutions such as the delivery of a number of containers together should be used.

044 | Used, damaged container/rusted container

Converting a container into a useful building mainly involves manual work: metalwork and welding to create openings and reinforcements etc., carpentry and insulation for the interior fittings, sealing of the roof and plumbing. The costs of this work depend very much on the degree and type of the conversion, and also strongly vary regionally and nationally because of differing pay levels. The total conversion costs can quickly exceed the cost of purchasing the raw container.

The following costs can be assumed for standard tasks: installation of a standard door approx. €750 (installation alone), installation of a window approx. €530 (installation alone), 80-millimeters inner insulation with particle-board cladding approx. €2,300 (20 feet), sepa-ration wall approx. €400, exterior painting in a RAL color approx. €800 (20 feet). These costs only account for the necessary openings in the trapezoidal sheeting and the use of reinforcements. The components themselves (doors, windows etc.) are not included in these estimates.

045 | Conversion of a container/work-
shop made of old containers
046 | above: block storages
below: first planned High Bay storage
system worldwide by DP World/SMS group

TRANSPORTATION

Regardless of whether piece items, bulk or waste materials, perishable, stable or toxic goods are to be transported—the use of ISO containers turns all goods into standard loads that can be transported together as part of a closed logistics and shipping chain.

The most important means of transporta-tion for containers is <u>transport by sea and waterway</u>. The largest container ship in the world is currently the Gülsun, owned by the Swiss shipping company MSC; it is 400 meters long, and 61.5 meters wide, and has a capacity of up to 24,000 TEU.[15]

The development of container transporta-tion over the last few years is characterized by continuous increases.

047 | Table: Container movements at the
20 largest ports in TEU units

Road transportation by truck offers advan-tages in terms of the quick, flexible final distri-bution of goods and thus ideally supplements shipping by water.

The interim storage in container terminals is currently carried out in block storages (stacking) with gantry cranes, where individual containers are hard to access. High Bay storage systems are a new development and operate like a high-bay warehouse, where individual containers can be directly accessed. There is a 200% increase in storage capacity predicted.

A 40-foot container must be securely locked to the chassis using twistlocks before being transported in this way. Variants of the standard chassis can have a number of locking points (to

secure two 20-foot containers), may have variable length, and may be able to tip the container or position it in a certain way.

A gooseneck chassis is a particularly flat chassis for high cube containers, which reduces the overall height of the trailer to a minimum.

048 | Container transport by truck

Container transport by rail is not as flex-ible as road transportation, but can be just as viable because of its loading capacity if the rail network is well developed and if suitable transshipment terminals are present. It is even possible to stack containers (two stories) for transport on freight trains, as is done in North America.

Test trains are now even traveling between Europe and Asia with the aim of eventually establishing a land alternative to shipping by sea. A German freight train from Hamburg to Beijing currently takes around 15 days, which is half as long as the same journey by sea.[16]

PRODUCTION

For a number of years now, the production of freight containers has been carried out almost solely in Asia—mainly in China, India and Indonesia. The reasons for this shift to production locations in Asia are the low wages and pro-duction costs and the proximity to Asian ports where exports dominate.

Containers are produced from prefabricated semi-finished products (rolled steel profiles, trapezoidal sheeting), which are then processed and assembled mostly by hand.

Because of the resulting fluctuations in quality, every container is generally subjected to various functional tests that check the stability, load-bearing capacity, watertightness and weight of the container.

Modern factories have a number of produc-tion lines. A production line can produce up to 70,000 units per annum, which corresponds to a frequency of around 8 minutes if uninterrupted production is assumed.

044

045

046

Year	2018	2017	2014	2008	2005	2002
Total TEU	347.900.000	334.200.000	300.180.000	247.422.079	183.300.000	113.400.000

047

2 x 20' standard container on standard chassis

40' standard container on standard chassis

40' high cube container on gooseneck chassis

048

Year	2011	2013	2015	2016	2017	2018
Total TEU	1.413.000	1.088.300	1.120.300	587.300	1.308.900	1.543.900

049

049 | Table: sales data of standard containers by manufacturer CIMC Ltd, according to annual reports

CONSTRUCTION

Freight containers are subject to extreme mechanical, climatic and chemical conditions during their everyday use. Repeated loading and unloading, lifting and lowering, and transport exposure to wind and weather in saline environments all make significant demands on the properties of the material used to make the containers.

For this reason, almost all freight containers are made of COR-TEN steel nowadays, a steel alloy whose name is derived from the two main material properties of CORrosion resistance and TENsile strength.[17]

Containers made of other materials such as aluminum, wood and plastics are less common as they have disadvantages in service.

For example, aluminum containers are significantly more expensive and less stable than steel containers, and are also more difficult to repair and convert as they cannot be welded.

Plywood containers with non-load-bearing wooden walls are less expensive than steel containers, but are not as stable or as resistant to moisture. In addition, their frames must be more generously dimensioned as the cladding is not load-bearing.

A frame made of various steel profiles welded to each other is the primary supporting structure. Different profiles are used depending on the position and loading involved: angle profiles, C profiles, rectangular profiles and even special cross sections with a sheet thickness of up to 4.5 millimeters. A secondary carrier-member grid provides reinforcement for the container base. The frame constructions are standardized in terms of type structures, meaning that no additional structural calculations are necessary apart from the compulsory loading tests.

050 | Detail of the frame structure

The walls of the steel container are made of 2-millimeters-thick trapezoidal sheeting that is welded into the container frame all the way around, just like the roof that is made of creased steel sheeting. Alongside its room-defining function, the wall-filling surface stabilizes and strengthens the frame and also bears loads from the supporting structure.

050

051

052

Because standard containers have a wall structure made from steel sheeting, their un-ventilated version will be vapor-proof; this can easily lead to the formation of condensate on the inside of the walls if the container is used as a building. This should be taken into account when converting containers into living quarters, as insulation is generally fitted inside the walls here.

So-called corner fittings are a common feature of freight containers. As the attachment points for loading, fastening and stacking, they are the basis of the overall transport system. For this reason, they are also dealt with by a separate standard (ISO 1161).

Corner fittings are made from cast steel and form the eight corners of each container. Every corner fitting is equipped with different openings on the three sides. The upper and lower openings, which are designed as slot holes to compensate for tolerances, are used for attachment when stacking containers; the side openings are mainly used for attaching the lifting and fastening equipment.

051 | Corner fittings
052 | Corner fittings

The base of a standard container consists of 28-millimeters-thick, 19-layer plywood sheets that are screwed to the cross-member grid. The sheet thickness can vary depending on the loading. Plywood bound by phenol resin is used here because of its resistance to both pressure and moisture. However, these sheets are not 100% moisture-proof, meaning that contamination with chemicals or fuels and the resultant vapors later on cannot be excluded in the case of used containers.

The opening at the ends for loading purposes is closed off with a two-leaf sheet-covered steel frame door. The door leaves can be opened through 270°, meaning that they can be positioned parallel to the side walls. Each door leaf can be locked using two bolts and corresponding supporting devices.

The seals on the container doors are made of EPDM, a synthetic rubber that has good elasticity, weather and moisture resistance, ozone resistance, and good thermal and chemical durability.

The COR-TEN steel surface is extremely resistant to weather and corrosion. The iron oxide layer that forms on an untreated surface is not permanent, however. If additional surface coating is not carried out, particles continually detach themselves from the corrosion layer, which would seriously detract from the performance of the container.

For this reason, containers are given a highly durable, epoxy-based, three-layer corrosion and paint coating. Damage to the coating cannot be avoided during service, but is not harmful thanks to the high steel grade.

There are hardly any limitations with regard to the choice of color. Shipping companies or renters often use the containers for advertising purposes and add their own corporate design. The result is the familiar colorful appearance of container ports and ships.

TECHNICAL EQUIPMENT

Containers are fitted with additional technical equipment as required. For example, cooler containers have permanent or retrofitted coolers (clip-on-cooler) that are connected to the electricity supply during storage or transport by sea.

057

053

055

054

056

058

They can also be operated using combustion motors while the containers are being transported by land. Mechanically ventilated containers are supplied in a similar manner.

Other items of technical equipment are confined mainly to transportation and transshipment technology. Technical equipment for security and for locating containers (GPS) has become increasingly common in recent years. Containers are fitted with chips that record and process identification and other data regarding loadings, contents and routes. In addition, modern container terminals have comprehensive security equipment to monitor and identify containers from the outside.[18]

Transport-specific equipment is only relevant for building use in specific cases; conventional heating and electricity supplies can generally be retrofitted.

SECURITY

Containers are securely attached to each other and to the substructure using corner fittings to provide optimum security for loads. This also applies when containers are used in building applications.

So-called twistlocks are used to connect the containers vertically and to anchor them to the subsurface in question; the twistlocks are inserted into the slot holes in the corner fittings and locked by turning the lug through 90°. Semi-automatic and fully automatic locking twistlocks are now in use in sea transport, which lock and release when they click into the corresponding fittings on the containers already present.

053 | Twistlock
054 | Vertical load distribution

So-called bridge fittings are used for horizontal connections in the lateral and longitudinal directions, bridge fittings connect two containers to each other using a threaded rod at the corner fittings. Bridge fittings are also used to transmit horizontal building loads (wind forces).

055 | Bridge fitting
056 | Horizontal load distribution

Various fastening systems are used to securely fasten containers in place on container ships, depending on the requirements. Rail systems for wall attachment are used together with base fittings that fasten the bottom container to the floor of the ship. Freely standing stacks of containers are strapped and attached to each other using lashing systems.[19]

057 | Lashing system/detail shot of lashing procedure/container being lashed
058 | Diagonal reinforcement using lashings

059

TYPE 2
BUILDING CONTAINERS

059 | Building container system

DEFINITION

The development of the building container involved the transferring of the concept of standardization and rationalization to a building module that would have the characteristic features of a freight container. The result is a prefabricated spatial cell module that is designed solely for building purposes and thus has a lighter structure.

STANDARD

Unlike a freight container, a building container already fulfills the civil engineering requirements demanded of a building envelope. However, it is a mass-produced item too, just like the freight container. In order to produce building containers as economically as possible, a standardized version in terms of fittings and structural design was developed that has established itself as a building module for short-term interim solutions.

The primary supporting structure of this standard version is made from steel profiles.

060 | Prefabricated steel components for container frames (photos from production at Kleusberg, from the company's Wissen site, Germany, hereafter referred to as Kleusberg)

The steel frame as a primary supporting structure is filled with a secondary supporting structure made of steel carrier beams that support the wall, floor, ceiling and roof fittings. The insulated surface fillings have a layered structure and an intermediate standard of thermal, moisture, fire and noise protection. They already contain openings such as windows and doors. Building containers are produced with a degree of prefabrication of up to 100%.

They leave the factory ready to be put into service.

061 | Primary and secondary supporting structures (photo: Kleusberg, Germany)

Special versions of building containers use alternate materials in their supporting structures, such as aluminum, stainless steel, wood/glued laminated timber or fiber-glass-reinforced plastics.

The addition of a building container module leads to redundant double structures—e.g. with regard to the wall, floor and ceiling fittings—which are unnecessary from a structural design point of view. The advantage of standardized mass-production should be weighed up against the disadvantage of the space lost when combining modules. Fillings can be partially omitted in order to create spatial connections between individual elements. Openings in surface-forming components are only possible to a limited degree as the secondary support structure, which is necessary to ensure the stability of the frame, will then also be missing. Because of structural stability requirements, the basic module consisting of individual containers, always remains intact in a multi-story construction made of building containers; this basic module also determines the layout of the interior space. For this reason, larger joined-up spaces are only possible to a limited degree.

USE

If one considers the purposes of building container constructions, they are most often purely functional buildings that are used as an interim solution until a permanent extension is eventually built. Building containers can be used flexibly to the extent that they function as

060

061

062

063

064

065

single rooms as all room-delimiting components are already present, but can also be combined to form multi-story buildings up to a maximum of 3–4 stories.

With their cell-like structure, these modules are suitable for layout systems with small rooms, which are then joined together. These buildings can be used for offices and administration, educational facilities (e.g. schools, kindergartens, and crèches) or medical facilities (e.g. laboratories, hospitals and mobile clinics, doctors' practices, intensive care units, ordinary wards).

Other possible uses for building containers include temporary accommodation (e.g. student accommodation, residences for asylum applicants, emergency accommodation in disaster areas), building site facilities (e.g. construction offices, storage and sanitary facilities) or technical equipment (e.g. equipment and air-conditioning containers, cooler containers).

062 | bbn – bed by night / Professor Han Slawik, Hanover, 2002

Building containers are also used as facilities for events, temporary sales buildings (e.g. ticket boxes, kiosks, fast-food restaurants), services (e.g. ATM machines), for information purposes (e.g. information stands, gatekeepers' buildings) and for presentation purposes (e.g. trade fair stands).

063 | seven-day architecture / LHVH Architekten, Munich, 2004
064 | derCube / LHVH Architekten, Freudenberg, Germany, 2007

Military applications are a particular area of use for building containers. There is a wide range of variants in terms of structures and fittings for these applications, which are tailored to meet the special technical requirements involved.[20] Special designs with higher security standards are also possible.[21]

Building containers are also used for research stations. Building containers can be transported in a fully-equipped condition if the research station is at a location with poor accessibility that can only be reached using special transports. Conventional construction work is often not possible at extreme locations because of the climate conditions there. The installation period available on-site may be so limited that the use of prefabricated modules is the only way of erecting a building during a certain time of year.[22] However, a second envelope must be provided around the building in the case of extreme climate conditions, as the thermal insulation of the building container will not be sufficient to buffer very high temperature fluctuations.

065 | Indian research station, IMS-Ingenieure and bof architekten, Antarctic, in progress

067

068

069

corridor in container

corridor container

066

TYPES

Standardization that involves various types as universal solutions has become established in order to allow for industrial mass production. Building containers are thus available with various layouts and fittings. These are defined by manufacturers in terms of their uses and are even categorized into product lines.

The basic type is "one room" or "one room with additional room". These are standard office cells that are 20 or 40 feet long, and are either with or without an additional room (for filing or for sanitary facilities).[23] In the case of the "multi-cell room" basic type, a number of office cells are combined to create a large open-plan space or a number of individual offices. This combination can also be used for shower or bathroom facilities with a number of cells.

066 | Floor plan variants for one-room/ multi-cell building containers

The stair container is used to provide access on multi-story buildings. It can be combined to create a multi-story stairwell.

067 | Production of a stair container (photo: Kleusberg, Germany)

Corridor areas can either be divided off using light walls or else created using corridor containers. Corridor modules may have differing dimensions (e.g. 1.5×2.5 meters or 1.5×5 meters).

068 | Corridor containers (photo: Alho, Germany)

A large number of special components are available that can be fitted to building container constructions. These include podiums, canopies, exterior ramps, corridor roofs, advertising boards on parapets, sun-protection lamellae and canopies to protect against sun and glare, fly-screens, additional sun-protection roofs, container roof platforms with rails and window flaps, and window security grills with clamp attachments. Roof reinforcement is necessary for more sophisticated roof fittings such as the planting of roof greenery.

The auxiliary technical equipment available includes air-conditioning and heating equipment (electrical indoor heating, gas or oil radiators—only when there is ventilation to the outside air), electrical installations, sanitary facilities, safes, equipment cabinets, sewage tanks and lifting equipment; these are either fitted to the outside (heating systems), slid under the containers (sewage tanks) or else positioned in a separate container.

Suspended ceilings with integrated lighting, floor reinforcements and raised floors for computer equipment can also be added.

069 | Utilities connections (photo: Kleusberg, Germany)

Some manufacturers offer building container systems with higher standards.[24] These systems have improved thermal, noise or fire protection, for example. Convenient room sizes, more generous facade design and interior fittings with higher-quality surfaces are all possible.

070

DIMENSIONS

Building containers were generally produced in line with the ISO dimensions that apply to transport containers. However, since manufacturers employ their own systems for production, transport and installation, it is also possible to use different dimensions that result in larger rooms, for example. These are based on the metric system instead of using dimensions in feet. In this way, the dimensions specified in the ISO standard have been extended. Building containers are not covered by an internationally binding standardization system.

The most frequently used <u>standard version</u> is the 20-foot building container. Other commonly used dimensions are 10 feet and 40 feet. Alongside the standard exterior width of 2.45 meters, there are also special widths of 3 meters and 4 meters. The height of building containers varies between 2.6 and 2.85 meters. For a height of 2.6 meters, the amount of head height available is only 2.3 meters. Larger special heights of 3 to 3.5 meters are also available to provide more head height.

070 | Dimension grid for building
containers
071 | Table of dimensions for building
containers

CONSTRUCTION

The primary supporting structure of building containers consists of a <u>basic frame</u> made of hollow steel profiles and rolled profiles; it is supported and reinforced by the secondary supporting structure as a substructure for the fillings. The welded steel construction consisting of the floor and roof frames is connected using four corner supports. The basic frame is pre-treated and either galvanized or painted to protect it against corrosion. Four corner fittings made of high-strength cast steel form the transport corners.

	Length ext.	Width ext.	Height ext.	Length int.	Width int.	Height int.	Usage area	Empty weight
10'	2,990 mm	2,438 mm	2,591 mm		2,232 mm	2,300 mm	6,5 m²	1,300 kg
20'	6,055 mm	2,438 mm	2,591 mm	5,852 mm	2,232 mm	2,300 mm	13,0 m²	1,950 kg
30'	9,125 mm	2,438 mm	2,591 mm	8,930 mm	2,232 mm	2,300 mm	19,5 m²	2,100 kg
40'	12,192 mm	2,438 mm	2,591 mm		2,232 mm	2,300 mm	26,0 m²	
Special width		3,000 mm						
		4,000 mm						
Special heights			2,800 mm			2,500 mm		
			3,050 mm			2,750 mm		
			3,500 mm			3,200 mm		
Special lengths on request	max. 12,000							

071

The fraction of steel in building containers is a lot less than in freight containers (the latter have around 70% steel). Fittings are responsible for a considerable portion of the self-weight of building containers. The relevant static loads that form the basis for sizing calculations for the supporting structure are the same loading scenarios that generally arise with tall buildings. These are the self-loads from the components, transport loads (depending on the type of use), and loads due to external influences such as wind, snow and ice. In addition, dynamic loading scenarios occur during transport and installation.

There are standard statics types for the sizing of building container constructions that already take all these loading scenarios into account. Project-specific statics calculations are only necessary in the case of special designs. Building containers can only be stacked up to a <u>maximum of 3–4 stories</u> because of the limited load-bearing capacity of the modules. The supporting structure is then <u>fitted</u> with wall, floor, ceiling and

roof fillings. The layered structure of these fillings varies depending on the level of comfort to be achieved. Once the frame has been produced, the fillings are created in the workshop largely by hand. The design of the fillings is precisely specified as part of the planning process. In this way, every container is tailored to fulfill a predefined usage. The amount of surface area occupied by window openings is relatively small for standard containers; these openings are implemented in the form of a perforated facade. Large-area, deep glazing is available in systems with a higher standard of fittings.

Galvanized crossbars that support a blind floor covering are included flush in the floor base as part of the <u>floor structure</u>. The floor is insulated with mineral wool and plywood sheeting is fitted on top of this, which then supports the homogeneous floor covering.

The <u>roof</u> consists of hot-dipped galvanized trapezoidal sheeting that is also supported by cross beams. These cross beams join up the frame structure to form a tortionally resistant unit. The roof takes the form of a trough roof, sealed using sheeting and then fitted with four roof inlets that are connected to rainwater drainpipes at all four corners. The roof is also insulated on the inside, fitted with a vapor barrier, and then covered with coated plywood sheeting.

The walls are finished using a profile sheet as an external sheet, which is then painted using a RAL color. The walls are insulated, fitted with vapor barriers, and then covered on the inside with coated plywood sheeting. Exterior doors made of steel are fitted to the door openings; the window elements are generally plastic windows with insulating glazing. The dividing walls are simple wooden- or metal-support constructions with insulation on the inside and cladding on either side.

> 072 | Wall-floor connection in a building container (photo: Alho, Germany)
> 073 | Ceiling-wall connection in a building container (photo: Alho, Germany)

PRODUCTION

Building containers are manufactured on a production line in 2–3 days in two main production steps: the first step involves the raw structure, while the second step deals with the fittings and finishing.

The steel parts are first cut down to size, derusted, and then welded to form a stable steel frame. The raw structure is complete once primer has been applied (production takes 2–3 hours per module).

> 074 | Welding the frame (photos: Kleusberg, Germany)
> 075 | Steel frame construction without fillings; rails and lifting equipment (photos: Kleusberg, Germany)

The fillings are then inserted into the frame. Horizontal surface elements (floor, ceiling) are first installed, followed by the vertical surface elements (walls). Window and door elements are also fitted as per the design planning.

> 076 | Surfaces being filled with thermal insulation (photos: Kleusberg, Germany)
> 077 | Installing windows and trapezoidal sheeting (photos: Kleusberg, Germany)
> 078 | Roof construction with drainage (photos: Kleusberg, Germany)
> 079 | Final coating of container modules (photos: Kleusberg, Germany)

Technical equipment is preinstalled or else fitted with sanitary utilities connections. Wiring is installed in each module and then connected for all modules later on. Interior cladding and roof seals are also fitted as part of the production process. The installation of fittings takes around 2–3 days. Rails and lifting equipment are used to move and rotate the container to aid the installation process. The container is ready for service once painted with a two-component RAL[25] acrylic lacquer or a plastic coating.

TRANSPORTATION

Building containers are fitted with devices necessary for transporting modules and fastening and connecting them to one another. Manufacturers generally transport their building containers on manufacturer-specific platforms whose dimensions are tailored to suit those of the modules. The building containers are fastened to the platforms using belts and special locks. They are then transported to the site and installed by installation technicians. Companies use mobile hydraulic cranes and installation transporters here. Building containers have crane lugs at the corner attachments that serve as lifting aids when installing containers using a crane. Two 20-foot containers can generally be transported on each truck trailer. Pack systems that can be taken apart represent an exception here, as they allow for the simultaneous transport of a number of building kits on a single truck.[26]

> 080 | Crane lug for crane installation (photo: Alho, Germany)

Building containers have corner reinforcements for the transportation of modules and the combination of spatial cells by stacking them; these reinforcements are comparable to the corner elements on freight containers.

Manufacturer-specific connection devices are available to securely attach spatial cells; they are similar to the rougher, more robust devices used on freight containers, but are much lighter.

> 081 | Vertical connection device (photo: Alho, Germany)

Building container modules are also linked together by means of utilities connections. Installation strands are combined over all the modules and then connected to the supply station.

> 082 | Utilities connection/electrical cable strand (photo: Alho, Germany)

072

073

074

075

076

077

078

079

080

081

082

VARIANTS

In order to minimize loads, light containers do not use a steel frame structure, but instead have stable wall, floor and ceiling elements. They are particularly suitable for installation on sites with poor accessibility. They also have a substructure that can be leveled. They can withstand being erected and dismounted at least 30 times, and can be installed by two people in 90 minutes without lifting gear.

Field camp containers are built in a particularly robust and stable manner, and their basic structure and walls are made of steel. The fillings are welded to the frame so as to create a seal. The metal components have long-term corrosion protection. As their name suggests, these containers are manufactured for use in field camps.

Folding containers have light structures and also save on space as they can be dismantled for transportation. They are also made of steel, just like standard building containers. When folded together, they are around 70 centimeters high. In line with their special function, they are suitable for quick, flexible use for applications where space savings during transportation are an important consideration.

The principle of the folding container was used in the "flexotel" in the Netherlands. The concept involves hotel-room units that can be erected at any given location desired. They are generally used for temporary guest accommodation for events. Structurally, this container is similar to a building container, but has the special feature that it can be folded together. It is fitted with freight container corners rather than with the corners typically found on building containers. Two units make up a single hotel cell. When folded together, the containers can be efficiently transported as a number of units can be packed onto a single truck. These are then "folded out" again on site using a crane.

083 | Folding containers/foldable hotel unit

Extendable containers (3-in-1 system) are the same size as a standard container when folded up. These building containers can then be extended on site using a folding mechanism. Installation only takes a few minutes. These extendable units include a 2-in-1 version and a 3-in-1 version, up to a maximum of a 4-in-1 version.

084 | 3-in-1 version of the extendable container

CONSTRUCTION PHYSICS

There are inherent structural weaknesses in the building container system. The high thermal conductivity of steel means that there are thermal bridges where the insulation is interrupted or reduced by the structure. This occurs mainly at the corners of a building container. In the case of permanent usage, this can lead to reduced comfort and to damage caused by moisture. After a longer period of service, leaks in the roof can also be expected.

These structural disadvantages are tolerated in the case of building containers so that the detailed solution used can be kept as simple as possible. Building containers are generally more suitable for temporary usages because of these weaknesses. An insulated building container still represents a significantly better civil engineering solution than a converted transport container.

Alongside regulations regarding thermal protection, there are also other guidelines that specify fittings standards, particularly in the case of workplaces. A minimum standard of fittings is necessary in order to fulfill these requirements.[27]

Production is subject to predefined quality standards. The warranty period for building containers is not uniformly regulated and it can vary depending on the manufacturer (1–2 years).

ECONOMIC ASPECTS

Certain manufacturers provide production, development, rental, sales and service for finished containers as a complete package: they carry out all tasks including consulting, planning, permission from the authorities, as well as construction itself and management of construction. The end product is then a turnkey facility that includes building services equipment, installation and interior fittings, which can be either bought or rented. Depending on the size of the order, the production period is around 4–6 weeks. Furnishings can also be provided as an additional convenience for clients. Manufacturers' websites feature detailed information with price-calculation tools, online planning systems and customer hotlines. Alongside rental and purchasing, manufacturers also offer financing, rent-to-buy, repurchase, and leasing.

Building containers are maintained and repaired in the workshop every time they return from rental use before being rented out again. Certain companies also have depots that can be used to store containers. Rental containers are subjected to regular checks. Every container returned is first given an "in-check" before being cleaned and stored in the depot. Containers are cleaned on cleaning lines in the workshop. A logged "out-check" is carried out when the container leaves the depot in order to document its condition.

The cost of a structure made of building containers is around 30–50% of that for a conventionally built building, on average. The costs are lower for containers placed in larger halls as they do not require climate shells.[28] The issue

083

085

084

086

of whether it is better to buy or rent a container depends on the requirements of the client and on the planned service life. Some manufacturers prescribe a minimum rental period of between three months and one year. The average service life of a building container is around 15 years[29], and even longer lives can be achieved for light structures at permanent locations. Once the service life has expired, the building containers are sold to countries where used containers are still in demand.[30] Containers no longer fit for use are recycled to recover their materials of construction.

The cost of a building container depends mainly on the fittings standard used. Very simple rental containers cost around €10 per square meter per month, while more sophisticated variants cost around €30 per square meter per month, or more. Installation costs for erecting and disassembling containers are around €15–25 per square meter. At the end of the rental period, cleaning costs also arise depending on the amount of soiling. The total rent often exceeds the purchasing price for rental periods longer than around 36 months, meaning that purchasing is the more economic option. However, this should be checked on a case-by-case basis.

New building containers cost between €550–750 per square meter, meaning that a 20-foot container costs between €5,000 and €10,000. Used versions of building containers cost around 50% of the price of new containers. However, it should be considered when buying containers that the purchaser will also have to bear disposal costs later on.

SPECIAL FORMS

Standard building containers have particular disadvantages with regard to architectural design and room quality. For this reason, the manufacturers of standard modules also include systems with a higher standard in their product ranges, although these have not proved competitive on the market so far. Room modules similar to building containers with alternate materials,

designs and dimensions can also be found on the market. They can all be broadly classified as building containers as they are modular, spatial-cell systems that can be transported in the same manner as freight containers.

Generally, these special solutions are tailor-produced spatial modules that have been developed for a particular project. The potential of these individual solutions is very promising with regard to the future development of building container systems as a high-quality architectural solution.

085 | HomeBox / Professor Han Slawik, Hanover, 2008

A comparison of the situation worldwide reveals that the types of building container on the market vary from country to country. For example, office and living containers are widespread in the USA—these are so-called trailers that already have their own chassis and function as mobile units. Their wheels are generally removed once they are in place at their final location and the trailers are then mounted on fixed foundations. The gap between the ground and the trailer is blocked off by an apron.

These trailers are used in the same way as building containers in Europe, and are made of wood and cladded using aluminum sheeting. Unlike building containers however, they cannot be stacked, and can only be combined horizontally. Thus, they do not count as a building system.

The use of trailers as both offices and homes is not unusual in the USA. Some Americans live in "trailer homes" that are either mounted individually or else as part of temporary estates. The lack of insulation, poor-quality and leaky windows give trailers a negative reputation of being inferior homes.

086 | Trailer, USA

087

TYPE 3
CONTAINER FRAMES

TYPE 3A:
Modular frame systems

087 | Modular frame construction method

DEFINITION

In principle, the modular construction system with frame cells is similar to the building container system (TYPE 2). The supporting structure of the modules is formed by a stable frame, just as in the case of building containers. It is industrially prefabricated in the factory as a compact, mobile unit along with part of the fittings, and is then assembled at the construction site to yield an overall building. However, in contrast with building containers, the building's "finish", which may consist of a weather-resistant building envelope or floor and wall coverings, is created and installed on site for all modules together. This means that a building made from module frames may take on certain design features of a conventionally constructed building. However, combination with conventionally produced components does reduce the ability of the building to be disassembled and reassembled.

Modular frame construction is significantly more flexible with regard to space, floor plan, and facade than previous container construction systems. Module frames are tailor-produced for the project in question, in line with the specifications ordered. Accordingly, the dimensions can be freely chosen here, although manufacturers also offer standard sizes that have proven to be suitable for certain usages. Although transport considerations do limit the maximum size of the modules, these dimensions can nonetheless still be quite generous as transport is carried out using custom-made platforms. It is not planned to integrate modular frame systems into the ISO-specified transport system, which reduces the flexibility of transporting modular frames. The dimensions and the fittings of the individual spatial modules are both

implemented according to the user's wishes with the required degree of prefabrication.

DEVELOPMENT

The first modular frame systems were developed as early as the 1960s. The impetus for the use of modular frame systems was provided by short-term increases in space requirements. Spatial-cell systems were mainly to be found in Europe and Japan. A Japanese company called Sekisui developed a fully independent construction system called "Heim". This was a system for building homes. Some German manufacturers of building containers, such as Ofra (temporary classrooms), Alho and Kleusberg, were also involved in these developments. They drew on their experience and expertise from container manufacturing and were able to use their existing production facilities and assembly lines in cases where modular frames were developed based on container frames.

Building using individual steel components that are delivered separately and assembled on site is much more widespread in the USA than in Europe. Systems based on frame cells are less common in the USA and have only begun to appear on the market in recent years. In Japan, however, spatial cell systems made of steel have been more successful than frame systems in the modular building sector. In Germany and the rest of Europe, the spatial-cell construction method is widespread, and wooden frames are becoming increasingly popular too as a cost-effective, long-term solution.

USE

Building using modules is most suited to repetitive building complex projects. For example, hotels are often built as frame

089

088

modules as they have a large number of identical rooms. Buildings based on prefabricated solutions also represent a cost-effective alternative to conventional buildings for schools, offices and administration buildings, laboratories, hospitals and multi-story residential developments.

The modular construction method allows for extensions and conversions later on. The supporting frame structure also represents a relatively flexible, adaptable spatial skeleton. For example, inside walls can be moved to a certain degree, even after a long period of usage, in order to alter the rooms to meet changing requirements.

Although individual room modules can be removed and reused, this does involve quite a lot of work due to the conventional components that have been added. For this reason, modular construction systems are mainly suited for permanent buildings.

DIMENSIONS

It is difficult to directly apply ISO container dimensions to universally applicable building modules, mainly because of their insufficient width of around 2.44 meters. A special width of 3 meters has now become established for building containers, as this makes them easier to furnish, even if it does also make transport more difficult. However, the dimensions of frames are determined by logistics and by production conditions. On the one hand, manufacturers' existing production facilities lead to limits on sizes connected with continuous production on assembly line trolleys; on the other hand, the dimensions are also limited by the transport vehicles used and by road widths. Dimensions of 20 meters for the length and 6 meters for

the width are actually theoretically possible for frame structures made of steel[31], if one were only to consider static constraints.[32]

Modular buildings generally do <u>not</u> have to fit in with a <u>predefined building grid</u>. Frames are tailor-made for the project in question and are available in widths that can be freely chosen between 2.5 meters and 4.5 meters, with room heights up to 3.5 meters and lengths of up to 18 meters.[33] System manufacturers also supply certain predefined module types. Since they can be combined horizontally and vertically, it is a good idea to limit the selection to standard types, meaning that <u>modules are combined as part of a system</u>. Within this system, the flexible applicability of the basic modules makes it possible to realize various floor plans and building forms.

088 | Dimension grid for module frames

PRODUCTION

The production principle is similar to that of building containers. The load-bearing frame structures are manufactured on assembly lines and equipped with largely complete interior fittings, including technical utility lines.

089 | Prefabricated frame cells
(photo: Alho, Germany)

In this way, frame cells with interior fittings can be produced with degrees of fabrication up to 90%[34]; however, the degree of prefabrication is only around 60% for the overall building on average. In contrast with the usual situation for building containers, components that are exposed to the elements, such as facade and roof, are installed on site for all modules together. This is also possible in the case of wall and floor coverings. This results in a combination of prefabrication and conventional construction methods. Some manufacturers also provide prefabricated and partially prefitted elements for the facades.

The high degree of industrial prefabrication and the ability to work independently of the weather in the factory can significantly reduce the construction period. However, the actual amount of work involved is determined by the quality and type of design desired by the user.

CONSTRUCTION

The main supporting structure is formed by the supporting frame with eight beams and four corner supports (superstructure). Depending on the requirements for fittings later on, the frame is fitted with a supporting substructure in the divider area. Floor and roof elements are usually made from profiles with varying thicknesses. Depending on the module length, it may also be necessary to use intermediate supports. Even though the main loads are supported by the frame, the additional secondary substructure is still essential. Steel has become established as the material of construction of the load-bearing structural elements. Systems with wooden or steel-bond structures are also available, however.

The modules are standardized, statically identical units that can be ideally adapted to their subsequent function and their role within the overall building. Clearances, stairwells and large, support-free room widths must all be taken into account during the manufacturing process. The individual room modules can be combined at their ends or longitudinal sides to create a complex supporting structure and, in contrast with building containers, they can be stacked to form up to six stories.

Although similar in terms of type and design, module frames are not as flexible as the system made from container frames that is described in the following. Adapting the frames as much as possible for the subsequent use makes it difficult to alter the existing building later on, as the additional supporting structures in the open areas mean that the fillings can only be removed to a limited extent.

090 | Prefabricated frame cells
(photo: Alho, Germany)

As part of the fittings to be carried out, fillings for walls, floors and ceilings are inserted into the open areas in the supporting frame structure. Light steel profiles with mineral fiber insulation, an inner vapor barrier and gypsum board cladding have become established as standard fittings for filling the external walls. Inner walls and ceilings also use drywall construction with supporting structures and planking. The standard floor construction consists of galvanized profile sheets with insulation and a floating dry screed on top of a supporting board. All building elements such as windows, doors,

interior doors, stairs and all building services equipment are delivered to the building site with pre-applied surface finish and are then mounted.

The facade is usually mounted on site too. This involves a continuous insulation layer in accordance with the relevant building physics requirements, with plaster or facade cladding, and with back-ventilation if necessary. The continuous facade, which is common to all modules, covers the entire frame structure and thus minimizes the thermal bridges.

The roof construction with sealing is realized with a liner sheet that is fitted as a sub-roof and a protective roof that can be freely selected and is fitted on site. With the modular construction method, a range of roof forms such as flat roofs with slope insulation, monopitch roofs, gable roofs or arched roofs in various materials are possible.

TRANSPORTATION

Construction begins by creating the foundation at the installation site. Flat-bed trucks transport the modules to the building site, where they then need to be mounted and connected to the electricity, water and sewage grids.

The modules are generally mounted after a planning and production period of around eight weeks. Although installation of the spatial modules can be completed within 2–3 days, it still takes a number of weeks for all fittings, finishing and for mounting of the facade. The units are thus generally ready to be used 10–12 weeks after being ordered.[35] However, the actual construction periods depend on the scale and design of the project in question.

Unlike other container building systems, module frames generally do not have transport openings at their corners. They are transported on the manufacturers' own vehicles, and are secured using tension belts. These are often oversized transports because of the sizes of the frames involved. However, ease for transportation is only of secondary importance for this system. Once transported to the building site, the modules are fixed in place, and are then joined up using conventional means, without the use of special attachment devices. This reduces their mobility and means that they can only be considered as a container-like system.

091 | Transportation and mounting of
spatial modules (photo: Alho, Germany)

CONSTRUCTION PHYSICS

The manufacturers' intention when developing the modular frame construction method was to develop a modular building system with optimal construction physics characteristics. Only in this way can unlimited applicability for these buildings be guaranteed without completely losing the advantages offered by prefabrication.

090

091

This adaptation to higher requirements was necessary in order to establish modular construction for applications outside of temporary usages. The increase in insulation thicknesses and the use of materials with better insulating properties were mainly responsible for the fulfillment of these requirements. The thermal bridges in the frame areas were avoided by premounting the building envelope.

In this way, buildings with modular frame construction systems can adhere to all requirements resulting from standards and construction law that are demanded of permanently erected buildings with regard to construction physics and noise and fire protection. The modular frame construction method also makes it possible to attain the standards achieved by conventional buildings.

ECONOMIC ASPECTS

The costs for a building erected using modular frame methods start at around €800–900 per square meter and can go as high €1,600–1,900 per square meter. These costs apply from the top edge of the foundation upwards; foundation costs should be considered separately. The construction costs are also strongly dependent on the client's specific wishes and on the finishing standard required for the building. In principle, this construction method results in lower costs mainly due to the rationalization of the building process and the associated shorting of the production process; the costs for the structure itself are approximately equal to those for a building of a similar standard built by conventional means. The modular frame construction system benefits from the advantages of modular prefabrication. Nonetheless, the disadvantage of high material use due to the redundant doubling of certain components still exists, and money cannot be recovered by reusing components either.

ECOLOGICAL ASPECTS

In terms of ecological efficiency, modular frames are not particularly favorable. Re-usability is very limited, as certain components are added to the mobile, prefabricated spatial cells in a conventional manner and would have to be produced again in the case of reassembly of the structure at a new location. The removed building elements, such as the facade, have to be disposed of.

The flexibility and variability of a construction system should also be considered according to environmental considerations. In this system, the secondary supporting structure is essential, meaning that the modules are not as flexible as a completely free system with non-load-bearing fillings alone, such as the system with container frames. In general, it is not possible alter the building with modular systems (except for moving inner, non-load-bearing walls).

MODULE CONSTRUCTION

Since the dominant temporary way of container construction has fallen into disrepute because of the banal rows and stacking, the manufacturers developed this design. Based on the frame construction systems, it is also suitable for permanent construction and called from then on modular construction. Technically, modular building is a generic term. This mainly refers to building with room modules and offers numerous possibilities, both in the configuration of the modules as well as for facades. However, some manufacturers want to make the modular construction all-rounders and imitate the conventional construction with facades. In the process, industrialized modular construction can create its own design-architectural language—but there are economic and creative limits. Draftsmen and designers are bound by an orthogonal grid and a strict geometry, which, however, can also be seen as a positive aid. There are also limits to logistics and assembly at construction sites in dense inner cities. In recent years, this type of modular construction has gained more acceptance and its share of the total construction volume is increasing. A decisive factor in this development is the fact that while manufacturer-layouters determine the building and urban-planning configurations, architects and urban planners are also hired— as it the rule in conventional construction. Steel structures have dominated so far, but wood and hybrid constructions (concrete and wood) have also established themselves with considerable results. It is always required to use automotive engineering as a model to produce the room modules. But an automobile is a self-contained and optimized unit. However, room modules are differently configured in one unit and only then become a finished building.

092

TYPE 3B:
Container frame systems

092 | Container frame system

DEFINITION

Against the background of the container building systems (TYPE 1 and 2) described so far, the idea arose to create modular building system that was as flexible as possible in terms of spatial, structural and design considerations, with a high degree of prefabrication and which, like the systems discussed so far, would also be based on the container principle.

There are already similar systems on the market from various manufacturers, but they generally only have limited flexibility and variability: the fillings can only be moved laboriously and with statics limitations, as they always perform a load-bearing function too. Certain components become redundant when the modules are combined (double walls, ceilings and floors), which increases the amount of materials needed and results in wasted space.

In order to optimize the container construction approach, the author of this book, Professor Han Slawik, developed his own building system using container frames. The result was the idea of separating the load-bearing frame from non-load-bearing fillings, i.e. the separation of supporting structure and fittings.

This system with container frames is currently still in its development phase and is mainly intended as a demonstration of the potential of modular building systems based on container frames. It is planned to build prototypes together with cooperation partners that can be used in smaller units and also combined to form larger building structures. This self-developed system has already been used and refined as part of various studies and competitions. This building system has already been patented.

DIMENSIONS

Two particular features of this building system are that it adheres to the preferred dimensions specified in the international ISO standard, and that the transport corners are fitted with devices that allow both for transportation using standardized transport equipment, and for the modules to be easily connected to each other. Additional attachable modules with the same dimensions as standard ISO modules are possible for various uses, such as access zones, service units (sanitary rooms, small kitchens), storage rooms, conservatories, etc.

USE

Various building structures can be achieved using the supporting module. The room-delimiting elements can be used to create rooms of varying sizes and heights. Different room layouts can be implemented depending on the usage requirements—e.g. as an office, studio, atelier, workshop, laboratory or (temporary) accommodation. This ensures variability in the fittings and flexibility with regard to uses, i.e. the continuously changing needs and habits of the users are taken into account and it is possible to alter the rooms to suit changing circumstances.

CONSTRUCTION

A supporting frame made of steel tubing (square or rectangular) forms the supporting structure; depending on requirements, this frame can also be made of aluminum or wood (glued-laminated timber), or of prestressed concrete rods or composite materials. The container frame supports the entire load of the building and is therefore more generously sized than the frame of a building container or a module frame.

093

095

094

093 | Facade in front of a one-piece
frame (variant 1)
094 | Facade mounted flush in a ther-
mally separated frame (variant 2)

The frame filling is available in two variants: with the first variant, the facade is fitted in front of the frame, meaning that the frame is covered over by the facade elements. This construction avoids thermal bridges, and the outer dimensions of the filled frame are increased by the insulation thickness of the facade elements. Under certain circumstances, transportation can be restricted when a premounted facade is present. The profiles of the supports and beams can be one-piece items.

The facade is installed flush with the surface in the second variant. The modules remain fully transportable and can be moved more easily later on. However, thermal separation of the container frame components is necessary in order to have the wall fillings at frame level. To achieve this, the supports and beams must be made of a number of smaller parts. There are various ways of achieving thermal separation. Concept studies on this subject will be continued together with cooperation partners as part of the next project phase.

In supporting frames, the frames are not load-bearing and act as simple room-delimiters. This means that freely selectable spatial connections can be created in the horizontal and vertical direction within the frame structure. It remains possible to remove and remount the frames and fillings, and the fillings can be altered independently of the supporting structure. This means that structural alterations that do not involve excessive labor or costs can be carried out during the construction phase or else

later on. The doubling-up of surface-forming components (such as walls, ceilings etc.) does not occur with this system. As with the previous systems, production can be carried out in a workshop in order to minimize the construction time on site.

095 | Finishing the frame modules using prefabricated elements (walls, floors, ceilings)

The fittings in the form of non-load-bearing, room-delimiting components (floors, ceilings, outer walls, inner walls) can be prefabricated according to standardized dimensions and then mounted, disassembled and remounted using a simple click system. Smaller elements and module-scale boards (e.g. wooden-frame construction elements) are all possible.

These elements can be selected as standard finished components from a catalog; however, the possibility of designing individual frame fillings should also be retained, e.g. by selecting specific materials and surfaces that are available from builders' providers. The simplicity of installation means that users will ideally get involved in the planning and building process themselves and introduce their own specific building materials for non-load-bearing room dividers (wall, ceiling, and floor). In this way, the building users will be able to make the building "their own".

As the container frames are combined with commercially available building elements, this is system can be considered to be an open building system.

096 | Combinations with additional modules

096

The flexibility of the building system allows for a wide range of combinations, including additional modules, and creates the basis for design freedom involving various materials, colors and surfaces. Horizontal and vertical interconnections and open spaces turn the mere stacking and arrangement involved in container construction into real architecture, with the help of these room-defining measures.

TECHNICAL FITTINGS

Installation connections are generally integrated into the walls in office containers, making it difficult to alter or replace them later on. For this reason, we recommend standardized and compact, rod-shaped elements with installation lines and plug connections to supply upper installation areas. Lower areas can be supplied using cable tracks, and it should also be possible to implement all circuits in a wireless manner.

If no supply and waste removal infrastructure is present on site, technical modules (power packs) on a modular scale (basic modules and/ or auxiliary modules) can help provide self-sufficiency. It should also be investigated whether rainwater can be collected and used as gray water.

ECONOMIC ASPECTS

The investment costs for a building system that offers maximum flexibility and variability will certainly be higher than those for the previous building systems. However, as this system is still being developed and is not yet available on the market, it is not possible to quote definitive data regarding costs. The more generously sized supporting steel frame has an influence on the costs. In particular, the costs for the solution with thermally separated frames cannot yet be quantified. For fillings, only the increased labor

costs for the reversible click system have to be considered as conventional building materials (such as sandwich elements) are used here in all other cases.

The investment costs must also be considered from a sustainability point of view. In this way, higher initial costs could pay for themselves over a longer period as significant investments for conversions, extensions, and even for reuse or new construction will not arise or will be more modest due to the ease with which the building can be modified.

ECOLOGICAL ASPECTS

From an environmental point of view, this is a very sustainable building system with great development potential. As with a modular system based on building components, all components are joined in such a way that they can be separated again, can be removed with minimal effort, used in different ways, or recycled. It is possible to react quickly to changes in the requirements demanded of the building or to changed usage circumstances: the size of the building system can be extended or reduced, if necessary. The inner walls are all non-load-bearing, and the ceilings too, only support their own loads and are ideally just as moveable as window elements and facade parts are. The flexibility of facade design makes it possible to achieve a varied appearance and to use materials that are favorable from an ecological point of view. The system allows for the facade to be renewed if damaged or if thermal insulation requirements become more stringent.

The service life of the building elements should be carefully considered: under certain circumstances, the support frame may still be intact after the fittings elements have been

removed and it could be reused as a basic frame. The potential of this building system is quite considerable from an economic and environmental perspective.

REMARKS

1 For example, a maximum width of between 2.5 and 3 meters applies for road transportation, depending on the type of road and the nationally applicable regulations. Objects that are wider than 3 meters count as special loads and must be accompanied by a suitably marked private vehicle in Germany and other countries.

2 The word "temporary" means "For a limited time, ephemeral, not constant; transient", source: http://en.wiktionary.org/wiki/temporary, as of: November 15, 2019.

3 Source: Lower Saxony building regulations 2012, "Genehmigungsfreie bauliche Anlagen und Teile baulicher Anlagen", Appendix 11: "Fliegende Bauten und sonstige vorübergehend aufgestellte oder genutzte bauliche Anlagen".

4 Transport of 20-ft-container by ship €0.07/km covered (2019, distance Shanghai-Hamburg is 12,079 km, approx. €840 excl. transfer, customs and other fees)

5 Cost of road transport of 20-ft-container by truck €1.80/km covered, 2019; special transport is more expensive.

6 Refer to the applicable depreciation write-off in Germany according to the depreciation tables at www.bundesfinanzministerium.de.

7 The purchase price for scrap steel is €90–140/t in 2019.

8 Kienzle.

9 Levinson, Marc; The Box; Princeton 2006.

10 As per ISO 668, from: Freight containers-ISO standard handbook; Geneva 2000.

11 DB AG (German State Railways).

12 TIS, the Transport Information Service of German transport insurers.

13 The container types are defined in the ISO standard and described in the following sources: Freight containers---ISO standard handbook; Geneva 2000 and Hapag Lloyd AG.

14 Survey of prices from various suppliers in October 2019 (Hansa-Container Hamburg, Renz GmbH, Conical GmbH).

15 www.spiegel.de/wirtschaft/unternehmen/mscguelsuen-in-bremerhaven-das-weltgroesstecontainerschiff-kommt-a-1282556.html, 19.08.2019 (31.10.2019)

16 Press release from DB AG (German State Railways) from January 24, 2008.

17 Rautaruukki Oyj, Rakennustieto Oy; COR-TEN Facades; Helsinki 2001.

18 Nikolaus, Katrin: "Wächter mit tausend Augen", in: Pictures of the Future, 2007, Siemens.

19 www.sec-bremen.de.

20 An example of a manufacturer in Germany is www.drehtainer.de.

21 Containers with bullet-proof designs (resistance class FB3) are also available to meet special safety requirements.

22 For example: Indian research station (bof architekten) or new Neumayer III building.

23 Special types, such as WC containers, are supplied in lengths of 5 feet or 8 feet.

24 For example: Alho basic plus, www.alho.com.

25 Special finishes in RAL colors are possible.

26 e.g. CS Transpack system, source: www.csraum.de.

27 In Germany: Workplace Ordinance (ArbStättV).

28 Hall inserts: Purchasing price approx. €320 per square meter.

29 In comparison: 50 years for a permanent building erected by conventional methods.

30 e.g. former Eastern-Block countries.

31 Stahl-Informations-Zentrum, Brochure 573, "Stahl im Wohnungsbau-innovativ und wirtschaftlich", Düsseldorf 2002, p.23.

32 Stahl-Informations-Zentrum, Brochure 548, "Kostengünstiger Wohnungsbau mit Stahl", Symposium, Dusseldorf, September 22, 1998.

33 According to: standard dimensions on www.kleusberg.de. The dimensions depend on the manufacturers in question. Wooden frame modules are only available at lengths of up to 14 meters because of their load-bearing capacity (www.induo.de).

34 Almost all module manufacturers advertise a degree of prefabrication of 90%; however, this always refers to the prefabrication of the modules with regard to interior fittings.

35 Construction period for an administration building with around 1,000 m² of usable floor area (www.alho.de).

STRUCTURAL DESIGN ASPECTS
GUEST CONTRIBUTION FROM THE ENGINEER DOUWE DE JONG

STRUCTURAL ENGINEERING AND FREIGHT CONTAINERS

In this part an approach is given as to how to calculate structures assembled with containers. Also covered is how to handle these units themselves and how to change or adjust the structure of these units according to their new purpose.

Building with units in general

Buildings assembled with freight containers must meet building codes and rules which are valid in the country where the building is going to be built. The building must also fulfill the requirements of the owner and the user. These requirements can be different for each project and will not be part of this chapter. We will not discuss foundations and other general parts of buildings outside the assembled units as staircases because in general they are the same as for conventional buildings.

Freight containers

Freight containers are self-supporting structural units. They are available in specified volumes and in many designs. Most of them are used as freight boxes. A worldwide set of rules and demands has been developed for these

containers concerning handling and shipping. Because of this standardization, shipping costs are lower when containers/freight boxes meet these specified requirements. These requirements are specified in International Standards. The only really standardized parts of these ISO standardized freight containers are the corner fittings, i.e. their exact place and the way they are placed. These corner fittings are mostly on the eight outside corners of the container, four on each side, and that is where the container meets the outside world. These standards are based on transportation and handling equipment. The other elements between corner fittings are up to the designer, and to the requirements of the client. Mostly these consist of a floor, two walls, a roof and a front and rear side, all within the space in-between the eight corner fittings.

ISO test loads and structural calculations

The requirements for containers are documented in so-called ISO (International Standard Organization) codes. An ISO handbook is available for freight containers in which a number of ISO codes concerning freight containers are

published. The requirements that each freight container must meet in order to be shipped in standard ways, and for the lowest possible shipping costs, are specified in these codes. When freight containers meet these ISO codes, they are marked as certified and one can expect that they perform up to the required loads, and within the required deformations. These ISO codes are valid in all ISO member countries, and authorities in those countries must accept the capacities for loads and deformations as specified in the ISO codes. The manufacturers of freight containers manufacture and deliver their containers according to these ISO codes.

By doing so, and by tests according to ISO codes, their product is certified. This is done by test loads conforming to the ISO requirements by accredited companies like Lloyds or other qualified suppliers. Structural calculations will be less specific than test loads, so a great part
of approving is carried out through test loads rather than structural calculations. And calculations give less result or ask for more material then the result of testing does.

When nothing is changed structurally in a certified freight container, it can be a building unit in itself. This gives every user or structural engineer specified information about the unit capacities for vertical and horizontal loads and deformation tolerance. Deformation is maximized for freight purposes and handling and storage tolerances for stacking. They can be calculated into elastic deformations and this information can be used to demonstrate building deformation requirements per unit. When stacking more units in heights or in a row, these units work together when structurally combined. Calculations of strength and/or stability according to the valid standards based on the steel specifications can also be made to demonstrate that a container building meets the requirements. But the outcome of structural calculations will most likely be less than the results of test loads. In a lot of cases, when new types of containers are developed or designed and the numbers are sufficient, test-load proof of required capacity will be used instead of structural calculation.

Assembling units

Building with containers means to assemble a number of units into a building or a structure. Assembling units means that connections are needed and these connections must be designed according the local building codes and the requirements of the client/user. The strength of these connections between containers in a building must be calculated, demonstrated, and designed according to local building codes and according to what is necessary for the actual building to be economic and safe.

Structurally assembled units

As with any building, vertical weight loads, and horizontal loads from wind, must be transported to the foundation, and/or outside bearings, and/or stability elements, by the designed structural elements. These are basic calculations and are the responsibility of structural engineers and designers of any kind of building all over the world. For standardized connections between containers and corner fittings, a number of shipping and storage parts are available and used by container companies during shipping, storing and handling. The capacities for loads and forces of these connecting parts are defined by their suppliers or manufacturers and are standardized and commercially available worldwide.

Design your own solutions

Every structural designer can design their own detail connections and/or reinforcements of existing containers to meet specified requirements of builders or clients. This can be a reinforcement of a column or a beam. Because of tolerances and temperature, deformation must be calculated so that the finished container building construction with units meets the local building codes and/or the specifications of the client. Bearing capacity of vertical loads and horizontal loads of each standard freight container are documented on a nameplate on the container and more detailed information can also be found in the ISO container specifications.

Adapting standard freight containers

Adaptations are mostly necessary when freight containers are used for purposes other than freight. After adaptation, the certification of a container is no longer valid with regard to its adjusted parts. The structural functionality of these altered parts must be demonstrated separately in order to ensure that the loads on the assembled building can be supported according to the local building codes. The same applies to deformation demands on the next unit, the foundation, or other structural elements outside the units.

When adapting containers—for example, removing the doors and the front side wall—a calculation of strength and deformation can be used as a way to demonstrate and guarantee that the structural unit complies with safety standards. The original parts of the container can be used as a framework with structural elements in software or hand calculations. If they do not meet the required numbers, additional structural elements as angle steel and/or box girders can be welded to reinforce the original parts in an efficient way. The requirements of the architect and the builders must still be met. The parts that are not changed keep their structural capacities or perform even better when reinforcement with additional elements is done. The changed part's stability can be demonstrated through structural calculations, and unchanged parts remain covered by ISO standards. When a sufficient number of units are changed, test loads on the changed unit according to valid ISO standards can save costs for material and calculations. The entire testing must be conducted in accordance with ISO standards or if individually organized, according to demands of the local authorities.

Conclusion

It is possible to use standard freight containers for buildings, when using the non-adapted structure capacity according to ISO specified loads as these are approved worldwide. The adaptations in the structure must be calculated for strength and deformation as standard. Testing adaptations of construction instead of calculations can often be rewarding.

This way, builders, owners and authorities can accept structural designs of buildings assembled with adapted containers as normal.

Structural engineers can design and calculate this way in what is asked for the container unit and also for the building. So engineers can use in their design the advantages of these wonderful containers.

07

PROJECTS

Project
PACHACUTEC HOUSE
Architect
TRS STUDIO

Project location   Pachacutec, Peru
Estimated use   Residential
Container type   Freight container

01

02

03

This conceptual design considers the shipping container as a solution for low-cost housing issues in Peru, taking the small town of Pachacutec as a case study. Much of the housing in this region is improvised, whereas TRS Studio suggests an organized, structurally sound alternative that fosters the entrepreneurial spirit of the local community. The proposal clusters two parallel containers per unit, topped with recycled poly-carbonate roofing, selected for its resistance to harsh weather conditions. Shipping containers are a viable option for their modularity and strength, as well as being a recycled material. Their standardized dimensions also simplify the architecture process to adapt the concept across different climates and contexts. The project is still in its experimental phase. The architects suggest that the first round of construction would prove a valuable learning curve to understand the replicability of the scheme. The ambition is for this project to evolve the urban image of Pachacutec as a beacon of long-term sustainable construction.

01
Single family dwelling concept, based on two cargo containers.
02
The roof is made from recycled cellular polycarbonate plates.
03
Front elevation.
04
Repurposed shipping containers were proposed for their ease of transport and ability to withstand harsh environments.

05, 07
The interior is built from
OSB recycled wood, which
is manufactured from wood
shavings.
06
Section drawing showing
interior layout.

Project
SCHMATZ TOKYO DOME
Architect
I IN INC

Project location   Tokyo, Japan
Estimated use   Beer stand
Container type   Freight container

The tradition of German beer halls is packed up and shipped to central Tokyo with Schmatz, a bar and restaurant in the Japanese capital. Housed in just two repurposed shipping containers, the volume's exterior signage glows, beckoning to passersby. Inside, the space is defined by solid wood, inspired by the traditional timber interiors of German restaurants and beer halls, and bathed in soft light with copper accents. Glowing orbs illuminate the beers on tap and add to the overall cozy atmosphere. The concept also takes inspiration from its positioning near Tokyo Dome, a stadium and home to one of the city's baseball teams. That explains the playful neon signage of sizzling hot dogs. I In Inc is a relatively young architecture partnership in Tokyo, whose founders strive to create surprising interiors that leave a lasting memory. Perhaps it is the contrast between the industrial exterior and warm, atmospheric interior, or perhaps it is the neon hot dogs, but the Schmatz beer stand is sure to leave guests smiling long after they have finished their last pint.

01

01
The charming interior of the beer stand.
02
The container's industrial surfaces are softened with timber flooring, warm lighting, and copper details.
03
Sizzling neon sausages and cheerful signage are among the playful details at Schmatz.
04
The beer bar, 28m² in size and glowing.

Project
DEL POPOLO
Architect
JON DARSKY

Project location   San Francisco, California, USA
Estimated use   Hospitality
Container type   Freight container

Perhaps the only thing better than fresh pizza is pizza delivered fresh. The Del Popolo pizzeria takes this a step further with its mobile pizza truck, a freight container on wheels kitted out with a handmade 2,268 kg Stefano Ferrara wood-fired brick oven and is mounted to the bed of a Freightliner M2 truck. With its hulking weight, the structure required a heavy duty truck to accommodate the load. One wall of the container has been replaced almost entirely with windows, which, when open, have what the designers describe as a "wingspan" of almost nine meters like a transparent awning. In the end, the truck does not just serve food, it is also a glass-enclosed exhibition kitchen, "seating" pedestrians and passersby at an impromptu chef's table. Aboard the truck, chefs churn out piping hot Neapolitan-style style pizzas to the pedestrian. Indeed, the pizzeria takes its name from the Italian words "of the people," chosen to reflect the egalitarian character of pizza. Now on wheels roaming the streets of San Francisco, the pizza is more accessible than ever.

01
This pizzeria comprises a wood-fired
brick oven in a modified container
set atop a Freightliner M2 truck.
02
The truck is a chef's table; one side
is filled with windows that open like
an awning.

Project
ILLY CAFÉ
Architect
ADAM KALKIN

Project location   Venice, Italy
Estimated use   Café and Bar
Container type   Freight container

01

02

03

Adam Kalkin designed espresso impresario Illy's café container, which was presented for the first time at the Venice Biennale 2007. The core of the container can be converted into a café, where guests may sit at a long table with a small library of books under a chandelier. The bar, with no less than three espresso machines, anchors one end of the container, and also conceals all the electrical wiring. To the left, a small workplace includes a desk and computer, and is adjoined by a washroom. To the right, the lounge consists of a sofa and side tables. The bright white interior was accessorized with a bright white awning.

01
Illy's coffee bar in the process of folding open via hydraulic mechanisms.
02
The bar closed after hours.
03
The bar fully open in the literal and architectural senses.

Project
PUSH BUTTON HOUSE
Architect
ADAM KALKIN

Project location   Various
Estimated use   Mobile home
Container type   Freight container

01

04

05

02

03

01–03
A view from the long side as Push Button house unfolds automatically—and in under one minute.
04, 05
View from the end of the container into the house as its walls fold open.

Just like the Illy Café, Kalkin's Push Button House unfolds like a flower at the push of a button. Here, the closed ISO freight container transforms into an single-unit home including kitchen, dining room, bedroom, living room, and library, by unfolding hydraulically. Beyond it's exemplary nature as a mobile home, the Push Button House became an artwork itself due to it's high level of transformation. In December 2007, Push Button House was exhibited in New York City where it welcomed holiday shoppers at the Time Warner Center. As part of the New York Wine & Food Festival, Push Button House again took center stage in the Meatpacking District in October 2008.

UNIQLO FLAGSHIP, UNIQLO POP-UP STORES

Architect

LOT-EK

Project location	Osaka, Japan
	New York City, New York, USA
Estimated use	Retail space
Container type	Freight container

01
Exterior of the Osaka
flagship.
02
A shop transported by truck.
03
Interior of a New York City
shop.
04
The exterior of a retail
container in the Soho
neighborhood.

01

02

03

For over a decade, the work of New York firm LOT-EK has exemplified the creative reuse of shipping containers, truck parts and tanks, along with other icons of the industrial world. For Japanese clothing retailer Uniqlo, the studio designed a 1,022-square-meter (11,000-square-foot) flagship in Osaka, Japan (that incorporated a single freight container into the building), along with pop-up shops in New York City. The pop-ups comprised two 20-foot containers that toured Manhattan to introduce the brand to the United States. Traveling on a knuckle-boom truck, these containers functioned as retail space, fully equipped with shelving, cash-wrap, and fitting room. Vertical windows aligned with shelving displays folded and anchored merchandise to the exterior. The fitting room was a custom-designed duct that gathered like an accordion towards the ceiling via a manually cranked pulley system. Linear bands of light illuminated the interior from both floor and ceiling while dressing mirrors lined both ends of the containers in order to visually elongate the limited space.

ETANIA GREEN SCHOOL
BILLIONBRICKS

Project location   Sabah, Malaysia
Estimated use   Education
Container type   Freight container

01

The Etania Green School is for stateless Indonesian children, whose parents came to Malaysia as undocumented laborers to work on palm oil plantations. The design team, the non-profit billionBricks in cooperation with Architecture BRIO, hopes this building prototype will be the first of up to 30 more schools of its kind. With space for 350 students aged five-13, Etania Green School is located beside a river that floods once a decade—a figure that is due to increase with the deforestation caused by palm oil plantations in the region. So whatever solution billionBricks proposed, it had to offer the children a safe place to access education and it needed to withstand floods. The vernacular architecture in this region is often raised above the ground, but the studio proposed placing the main timber structure atop five repurposed containers to shield it from high water. This allowed them to create a more stable foundation using fewer

02

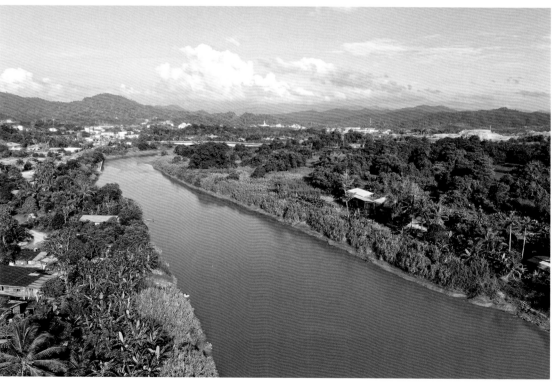

01
The Etania School uses freight containers to protect the building in case of flooding.
02
The river beside the school has an increased threat of flooding due to deforestation.
03
The containers themselves are used for storage and toilets.
04, 05
The classrooms.
06
Children can access the classrooms via ladders, as well as a central staircase.

components. Four classrooms, a teachers' lounge, and library are arranged in blocks across the upper floor on either side of a central veranda. Between two classrooms are two smaller areas for group work—one is a cozy reading room with a netted floor where the children can enjoy library books. These areas give the teachers additional space to hold lessons, as multiple years are often grouped into a single class. The building is also designed as a place of exploration, one that students can access in several ways: climbing a dirt mound, ladders or staircases. The ascent is an articulation of the school's ethos of overcoming obstacles.

PORT-A-BACH

ATELIERWORKSHOP

Project location   Various
Estimated use   Mobile home
Container type   Freight container

01

02

03

04

Atelierworkshop fabricated its one-room Port-a-bach vacation house from a single 20-foot freight container with an additional roofed area of 14 square meters (151-square-feet). When folded out, the inner room is supplemented with a terrace that runs along the longitudinal side of the structure and with balcony-like reclining surfaces at one of the container's open ends. Flexible furnishings can be stored in the wall. This and other efficiencies of organization mean that four people (two adults and two children) can comfortably inhabit Port-a-bach despite its minimal floor space. The house can operate in a stand-alone manner from a technical point of view, however, it can also be connected to existing public utilities (electricity, water, sewage) if necessary. The architects present Port-a-bach as a sustainable alternative to the vacation or mobile home because it can be removed without leaving any trace behind. This would suggest that entire caravan parks can be returned to nature in an easy and relatively inexpensive manner as the tourists move on to fresh destinations. Best of all, although the house is temporary and transportable on the one hand, it is also suitable for long-term and permanent use because of its robust construction based on the freight container.

05

06

01, 02
The container opens and closes easily, with beds and a deck folding or sliding outwards.
03, 04
When open, the terrace reveals the container's great space efficiency.
05, 06
The kitchen fits into a wall immediately adjacent to the fold-out bedroom.

CAMPUS
Architect
HAN SLAWIK

Project location   Almere, the Netherlands
Estimated use   Building laboratory
Container type   Freight container

01

02

03

04
05

01
The interior and view
through its floor-to-ceiling
(literally) window.
02, 03
Interior details.
04
Axonometric drawing.
05
Floor plan.
06, 07
Four updended containers support a fifth to form a tower.
08
To maintain the loadbearing
strength of the containers,
Slawik cut only minimally into
the boxes to create windows
and doors. Between the volumes, he made a light-filled
conservatory under large
swathes of glass.

Slawik designed a temporary home that would stand for five years in Almere as part of the local government's Temporary Living competition. Campus was one of only 17 entries selected to be built and was the only project constructed from steel shipping containers. Campus is considered by some to be the spark that initiated container architecture in Europe. The architect placed four 20-foot steel shipping containers vertically on the flat polder landscape to support a fifth that served as a small tower and determined the separation of the four boxes below it. The space between them was enclosed by a single glazing and could be used as a conservatory. Because containers are designed to support excess loading, weakening them by cutting openings into them during their conversion into housing was feasible. Nonetheless, Slawik cut only small square openings into the trapezoidal sheeting walls in order to avoid having to use additional reinforcement. Door openings were cut from the walls, fitted with frames, and then the original cut-outs were used as doors. The modular dimension of 2.26 meters, borrowed from Le Corbusier, formed the basis of Campus' interior planning grid, however, the 20-foot containers, by their nature, already lent an outward impression of order to the assemblage.

Project

FOGHOUND INTERACTIVE COFFEE SHOP & SHOWROOM

Architect

EARTHWORLD ARCHITECTS & INTERIORS

Project location   Johannesburg, South Africa
Estimated use   Hospitality/Coffee shop and showroom
Container type   High-bay freight containers

Earthworld have used seven high-bay, or high-ceilinged, shipping containers to create a coffeeshop and appliance showroom for Foghound, a South African coffee brand with sustainability close to its heart. The container's steel frames were mounted above a masonry foundation to create a warehouse-like office space in a quiet suburban area of Johannesburg. The vertically stacked containers create an open courtyard area. The pair of containers that host a first floor showroom cantilever over the ground-floor containers to create a cozy niche to house the coffeeshop. The space is filled with natural light, which pours into the lower containers through clerestory windows. Inside, the interior finishes are restrained in order to hero the container-based structure. A reclaimed timber ceiling and raw concrete floors were installed by the team, which are punctuated by Foghound's watercolor branding stenciled onto the container walls. As part of the brand's focus on sustainability, many of the furnishings and interior finishes throughout are salvaged or upcycled—a nod to the client, who is an avid collector.

01
The cafe steps up from a masonry foundation.
02
This cafe is for an eco-friendly coffee brand.

03
A stairwell links the high-ceilinged containers.
04
Daylight pours through large glazed openings.

CARROLL HOUSE

LOT-EK

Project location   New York City, USA
Estimated use   Residential
Container type   Freight container

01

02

01, 02
The diagonal volume built from
21 stacked freight containers.
03, 04, 05
Kitchen, dining, and
living spaces are found
on the first floor.
06
Two containers make up
individual bedrooms for the
children, with a large open
area for play.
07
The containers are stacked
to create ample outdoor
space along the rear of
the building.

04

05

06

07

On a typical Brooklyn lot, New York and Naples practice LOT-EK have constructed a less-than-typical single-family residence. Shooting out of the pavement like a monolithic diagonal beam, Carroll House is constructed from 21 stacked containers that are cut along the top and bottom. The result is a 232 square meter (2,500 square foot) diagonal volume where three of the four levels have a private outdoor space at the rear, shielded from public view thanks to the strategic cut of the container walls. The outdoor spaces are framed by large glass sliding doors, creating continuity between inside and out.

A downhill ramp at the front of the building offers access to the garage on the lower level, where the cellar is also located. Kitchen, dining, and living rooms are situated on the first floor, as well as a media room with a projector and bleacher-style seating. One floor up is a level dedicated to the children, where two bedrooms and a play area are each carved from a container. The main bedroom and en-suite is tucked away on the top floor.

08, 09
The diagonally cut containers
on the ground floor make
way for a ramp that leads to
the cellar and garage.
10, 11
Container walls frame the
terraces along the rear of
the house.

Project
KIOWA PROTOTYPE (HABITAINER)
Architect
LUIS RODRÍGUEZ ALONSO, JAVIER PRESA

Project location   San Antonio, Canary Islands, Spain
Estimated use   Private residence
Container type   Freight container

01–03
The end of the container opens out as a balcony but also, when the steel walls are partly closed, serves as a doorway.
04, 05
Drawings demonstrate how containers can be fit like drawers into a larger structure and supplemented with stairs and exterior windows.

01

02

03

04

05

In the Canary Islands, Spanish architects Luis Rodriguez Alonso and Javier Presa created this 14-square-meter (151-square-foot) residence from a 20-foot, steel ISO freight container, which serves as the home's structural chassis. The interior panel system is a composite of polyurethane, polystyrene, wood frame and medium density recycled fiberboard.

The architects painted the ceiling and walls a matte white and sheathed the floor with a seamless plastic finish, dubbing this sophisticated vessel for the containment of domestic life a Habitainer.

Project

MDU/MOBILE DWELLING UNIT

Architect

LOT-EK

Project location   Walker Art Center, Minneapolis, USA
                      Museum of Art, University of Santa Barbara, California, USA
                      Whitney Museum of Art, New York, USA
Estimated use   Mobile home
Container type   Freight container

01

03

02

01
By cutting into the container, LOT-EK created closable drawers to expand the interior and let in light.
02
Renderings show how MDUs arriving at a port can be loaded into a track and slid into place in a community of nomadic living units.

03
An interior view.
04
Floor plans show a unit closed for shipping (top) and open for living.

04

This is the new Plug-In City: LOT-EK's Mobile Dwelling Unit (MDU) is created by making incisions in the metal walls of a 40-foot cargo container to define extruded sub-volumes. In transit, these volumes are pushed in like drawers, allowing worldwide standardized shipping of the home. When in use, the volumes remain pushed out, leaving the interior unobstructed. Architects Ada Tolla and Giuseppe Lignano conceived of the MDU for the new nomad, enabling the residential unit to travel with its inhabitant like a vast steamer trunk, filled with the owner's belongings whilst en route. At its destination, the MDU is jacked into a multilevel steel rack by a crane that constantly loads and unloads MDUs into slots where they are anchored via steel brackets into assigned positions and plugged into local services. LOT-EK compares the units to pixels in a digital image, temporary patterns generated by the presence or absence of dwellings, reflecting the ever-changing composition of these modern-day international colonies.

BORNACK DROP STOP TRAINING CENTER

PATZNER ARCHITEKTEN

Project location   Marbach am Neckar, Germany
Estimated use   Training center and office space
Container type   Building container

01
Containers added more intimate space, for safety training, to this former steam power plant.
02
The new, but still industrial, stairwell.
03
The end of each container was fully glazed to give monumental views of the building's main volume.

For anyone—from elevator and bridge repairers and outdoor adventurers, to rescue squads and construction workers—Bornack offers bespoke security systems, coaching and consultation, as well as "drop-stop" safety equipment. Patzner Architects transformed a monumental, landmarked former steam power plant in Marbach am Neckar (built in 1939 and closed in 1951) into its fourth training and product development center. To do so, the designers tore out all the old coal boilers except one inside the boiler house, adding 500 square meters (5,382 square feet) of space over several floors to this industrial cathedral of 3,000 square meters (32,292 square feet). Patzner converted the factory into offices, training ranges, camps, and meeting and break rooms while working hard to reconcile the magnificent original structure with these new functions. By raising shipping containers 6.5 meters off the floor, the designers underscored the church-like volume and epic 35-meter ceiling height of the existing building (this is also emphasized by the new stairs which hang from two powerful old steel girders). By completely glazing the ends of the boxes, the architects punctuated the space with new layers of texture and transparency. Inside the containers, visitors seem to float in midair while enjoying a magnificent view of "the mountain climbers", clients who train in drop-stop safety directly opposite these windows. Patzner was wise to preserve the existing building strategically and generously, including rehabilitating concrete and steel surfaces, in order to communicate the original character and surreality of the plant environment.

Project
CONTIKI II
Architect
CONTAINERMANUFAKTUR

Project location   Woltersdorf am Kalksee, Germany
Estimated use   Commercial
Container type   Freight container

01

02

A shipping container finds a new lease on life ... aboard a boat. No longer destined to traverse international waters, however, this container micro-home concept is envisioned as a practical and contemporary living space. The mobile home is floating on the scenic Kalksee, just east of Berlin. The benefits are plentiful, argues the manufacturer of the 30-foot container home, chief amongst them being that it does not require a building permit. In Germany, more and more municipalities are rethinking their waterways and opening them up to allow boats and floating homes to dock.

The 20-square-meter (66-square-foot) home is cozy in the winter—especially with its well-insulated walls and underfloor heating—and expands to 60 square meters (197 square foot) in the summer when the wraparound terrace offers an extended living space. The interior is a bright and airy departure from the dark spaces typically associated with houseboats. Electricity, plumbing, and even internet access are all built-in, while a simple structure means the container can easily be removed from its base.

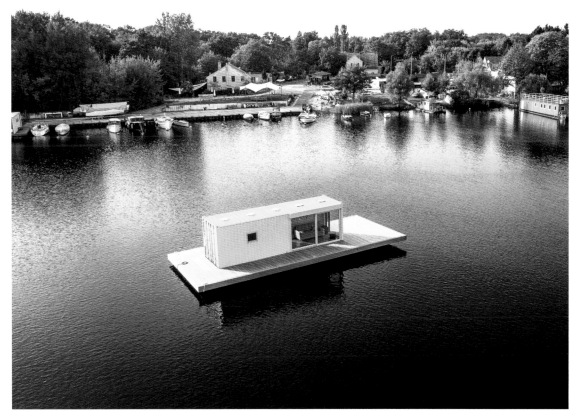

01
The light, airy interiors
are complemented by
the cheerful yellow paint.
02
An abundance of outdoor
deck space.
03
The substructure is made
out of polyethylene cylinders
connected to a steel mesh,
which enable the construction
to have a maximum terrace area.
04
The floating home is self-
propelled and fully mobile.

Project
THEATERHAUS STUTTGART
Architect
PLUS+ BAUPLANUNG
WITH ENGELHARDT.EGGLER.ARCHITEKTEN

Project location	Stuttgart, Germany
Estimated use	Event space
Container type	Freight container

01

03

02

This architectural reinvention puts a modern face on an historic landmark factory building, connecting two periods in time without disjunction. The architects suspended a freight container just above the main entrance that looks out onto the adjoining plaza, serving as a fine advert for the theater and creating a single windowed room. The energy-saving extension embraces the old structure (literally) while giving it both fresh purpose and authenticity.

01
Visible at the entrance: a container used in the renovation and the modern cladding placed over the old brick facade.
02
The entrance seen from inside.
03
The facade seen in cross section.
04
The facade seen from the plaza.

SKY IS THE LIMIT

BUREAU DES MÉSARCHITECTURES

DIDIER FIUZA FAUSTINO

Project location   Yangyang, South Korea
Estimated use   Tea house
Container type   Container frames

01

02

03

04

01, 02
The tea pavilion above
Yangyang.
03
Inside one of the pavilion's
twin containers, looking
toward the Sea of Japan.
04
The stairwell seen from one
of the container-rooms.
05
The containers hang 20 meters
above ground.

Along the shoreline in Yang-yang, South Korea, Sky Is The Limit is a 100-square-meter (1,076-square-foot) tea pavilion, suspended 20 meters above the ground overlooking the Sea of Japan. Didier Fiuza Faustino's Paris-based Bureau des Mésarchi-tecture projected this steel-framed tearoom above the horizon and lined it with varnished plywood, glass and steel duckboard. The building's body resembles a curious robotic skeleton,

a Japanese Wall-E, its thin tension-rod laced structure accessed by a series of staircases that lead visitors up to the creature's "eyes," a pair of generously open-ended viewing plat-forms made from container frames. The two voids, of identical dimen-sions, provide diametrically opposing views of the landscape below.

Project
MOBILE LIGHTHOUSE
Architect
ARHITEKTURA JURE KOTNIK

Project location   Paris, France
Estimated use   Installation and exhibtion
Container type   Freight container

01

01
The mobile beacon of
fluvial transport.
02
The top container housed
two beam headlights that
shone over the Seine.

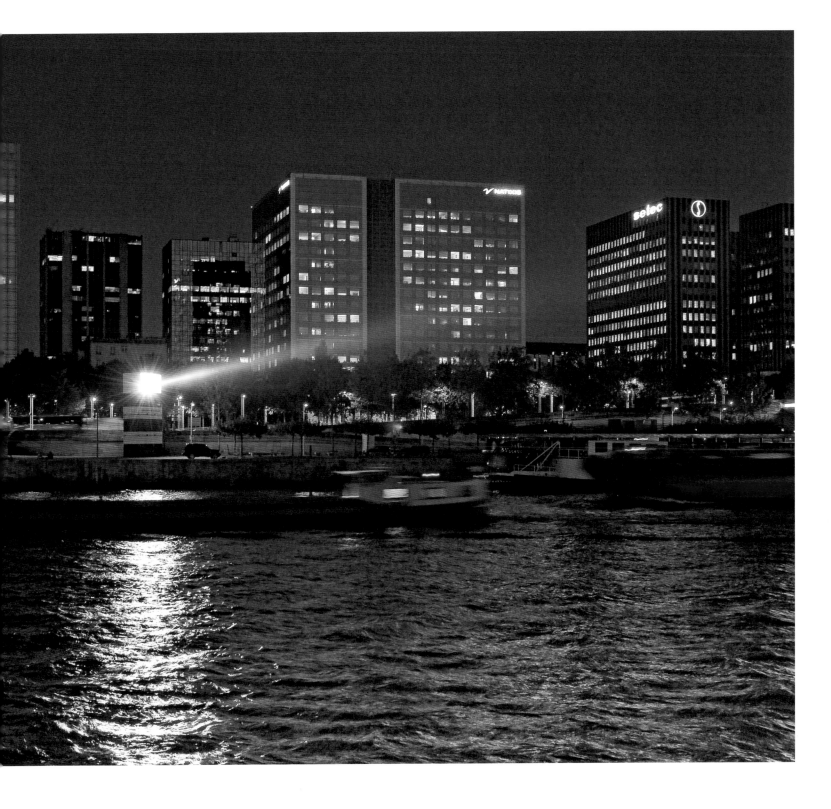

Landlocked Paris might not conjure up associations with being a major shipping center, but the French capital holds the second largest inland port in Europe, moving 20 million tons of cargo along the Seine every year. To commemorate the 40th anniversary of the Ports de Paris, the mobile lighthouse was commissioned, itself a beacon to fluvial transport as an environmentally friendly and carbon-efficient alternative to transport by road. The temporary structure combines two fundamental elements of shipping, one historic and the other a more recent follow-up: the lighthouse and the container. Four repurposed six-meter containers stood stacked on top of one another, the ground floor housed an information center and exhibitions about river transport, while the upper container enclosed two rotating beam headlights that shone over the city. The 10-meter-high structure traveled to five different riverside locations over a span of three months—a process easier to manage with prefabricated shipping containers.

BRLO BRWHOUSE
GRAFT ARCHITECTS

Project location	Berlin, Germany
Estimated use	Brewery, commercial, hospitality
Container type	Freight container

01

02

03

01, 02
Super graphics animating the
BRLO Brwhouse facade.
03
A screen installed for hop
plants to grow into a fragrant
green canopy.
04
BRLO describes its Brwhouse
as a "craft beer playground
in the heart of Berlin".
05
Containers are stacked vertically to contain a stairwell.
06
BRLO Brwhouse interior.

Berlin's Gleisdreieck Park is a success story of urban renewal: once an overgrown space between train tracks, it is now one of the city's most popular parks. In 2016, Graft oversaw the completion of a mobile brewery and beer garden—a place for gastronomy, events, beer brewing, and offices. The freestanding structure was inspired by the Platoon Kunsthalle buildings in Seoul and Berlin, which are composed of overseas shipping containers. At BRLO, the containers were used to create a mobile base for an envisaged duration of three-to-five years. Four side-by-side containers stacked three-high creates a 600 square meter (6,458 square foot) space for BRLO to accommodate its beer-brewing operations, offices, and to welcome guests. Another container stands vertically to house a staircase, while yet another stands on an angle to provide access to a gallery above the outdoor space. The starkness of the container architecture and the bold black and white super graphics on the exterior are softened by the landscaping program. In the beer garden itself, the brewery's hop farmers collaborated with interior design firm Novono to create a green canopy of fragrant hops.

Project

SPACEMAN SPIFF

Architect

SERDA
ARCHITECTS

Project location	London, Great Britain
Estimated use	Residential
Container type	Building container / freight container

01
Serda's renovated barge.
02
The container used to add
domestic space on the boat.
03
Interior detail.
04
Views through the newly
glazed container walls.

01

02

03

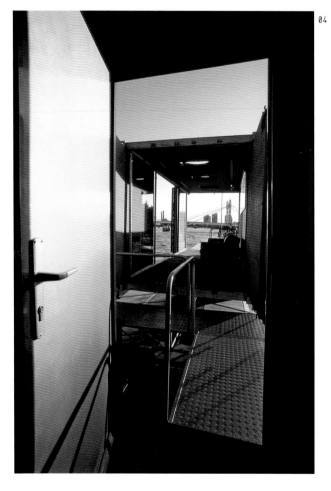

04

In the London district of Chelsea, directly under Albert Bridge, there's an inconspicuous old barge, the current usage of which can only be discerned when taking a look at its neighborhood that boasts white, elegant houseboats and yachts—for its outer appearance hardly changed after it was converted from a freight ship into a houseboat. Austrian architect Eduard Serda bought the inland freight ship, constructed in the 1960s, and converted it into a spacious, 250-square-meter (2,690-square-foot) residential ship in just five months. The core of the ship is the former freight compartment, which he transformed into a spacious living room.

Its ample space is enhanced by a roof that can be fully opened—a result of its original use as a cargo compartment. One freight container and two smaller prefab containers were installed in the cargo compartment to subdivide the space in a functional way. All three containers can be hydraulically lifted to the deck, where they are then living spaces that can be opened to the outside, or allow the entire living area to be used for other purposes.

06

07

05
Serda used building containers to
create his floating bachelor pad.
06, 09
The space into which bedroom
containers slide below decks
for storage.
07
A room lined with Japanese screens.
08
Sisal flooring mixes with
outrageously floral upholstery.

Project
HOMEBOX1
Architect
HAN SLAWIK

Project location	Various
Estimated use	Private residence
Container type	Building container

01
The movable home is fitted with steel corners for easy shipping.
02
Looking down the stairs.
03
In HomeBox1, floors are of equal heights.
04
Asymmetrical stairs make the most of very little space.
05
The kitchen.
06
View from the rear.
07
Slawik's highly efficient floor plan.

01

02

03

07

Professor Han Slawik's Home-Box shelters a miniature mobile house in a wooden container instead of the typical steel boxes in wide use around the world. Depreciation, repair and maintenance are all more expensive for steel (in terms of purchasing costs, welding, etc.) than for wood. A vertically positioned HomeBox requires little surface area and stands like a "nomad" on urban infill or rural sites and while clustered, through its repetition can create a new species of city fabric (a lane, path, street, or square). Slawik suggests that the dwelling could be used as emergency shelter or even, during major temporary events such as the soccer World Cup, an Expo or Olympic Games, erected as temporary container cities or villages to provide hotel facilities and lodgings.

HomeBox1 has three levels, all of equal height, whereas HomeBox2 has larger upper and lower levels; the mezzanine has a lower height and is intended as a sleeping level. The containers are designed to be independent of location, and feature a closed rear with a generously opened face. The supporting walls and ceilings consist of multilayered wood panels equipped with steel ISO corner fittings so that they can be transported by truck, train, and ship and set up using standard lifting devices such as cranes. The corners are screwed to the wooden walls with welded, perforated panels. Slawik's design ensures that not only the corners but even a single panel can support the entire box.

HOLYOKE CABIN

PAUL STANKEY, SARAH NORDBY

Project location   Holyoke, Minnesota, USA
Estimated use   Private residence
Container type   Freight container

01
The building and its
components.
02, 03
A pair of containers
flank a central roofed
timber construction.
04
A window in one of the
containers relates that
volume to the heavily-
windowed core structure.
05, 06
Interior details.
07
Each container has its
own foundation.

01

02

This weekend home in the small town of Holyoke, Minnesota, was built by Paul Stankey and Sarah Nordby, the couple wanted to replace a trailer home that had fallen into disrepair. The architects' goal was to come up with as permanent and robust a solution as possible on a tight budget, while investigating various construction methods and materials that would be able to withstand the extreme weather conditions over the course of the year. Because their hometown is located close to a container terminal, the two were inspired to use old shipping containers. This meant that the house would have all the basic functions of any other home, but in a minimal form: a kitchen, dining room, living room, washing and clothes area, and two beds. Stankey and Nordby transported a pair of 20-foot containers to the site and installed them on individual foundations to serve as the sides of the house. Between them, they placed a timber construction with generous steel-framed windows in order to provide sufficient lighting and support the projecting roof structure. The used shipping containers were hardly altered from their original form: apertures cut into the side walls link the containers to the central structure to form a common space, while narrow but strategically positioned window slits offer views of the surrounding landscape.

05

06

07

SAUNA BOX

CASTOR DESIGN

BRIAN RICHER AND KEI NG

Project location   Various
Estimated use   Sauna
Container type   Freight container

01

02

03

01-03
This movable sauna-in-a-box
can be situated anywhere:
a backyard, a backstreet,
or even a snowy clearing.
04
The existing container
doors swing open to reveal
a smaller, more traditional
door leading into the sauna.

04

This mobile, stand-alone architecture holds a traditional, wood-fired sauna that was built into a 10-foot steel container. The COR-TEN steel container has standard dimensions and components so that the sauna can be transported to any location without requiring a specially constructed site with specific utilities. An integrated wood oven, rainwater storage and rooftop solar panels make the unit self-sufficient. Aesthetically, it is marked by the interplay of its variety of materials: on the exterior, Castor clad the box with robustly weather and seawater-resistant steel; inside, the sauna is lined with warm wood that corresponds to the overall function of a sauna. The variety of materials is also emphasized by the furnishings that were selected, including stone furniture and wash basins, wooden and metal fittings and fixtures. When the sauna is in operation, the container doors swing open, enlarging the diminutive entrance where the oven opening,

a shower and seating are located. The sauna cabin itself, is finished with wood as is typical and has a window opening that, visible on the facade of the container, becomes clear evidence that this structure is not being used in the predictable manner. The architects refuse to mass-produce the Sauna Box, offering instead to fabricate each one to meet the specific requirements of each client, adding bespoke sound systems, guitar amplifiers, lighting or furnishings. The interior design is tailored to suit the advantages associated with the reuse of a freight container, in no way compromising the mobility that is the container's virtue.

Project
FUTURE SHACK
Architect
SEAN
GODSELL

Project location   Various
Estimated use   Emergency housing
Container type   Freight container

01

02

03

04

05

Looking like one of NASA's old Apollo lunar landers, Future Shack is actually a mass-produced relocatable house that can be assembled within 24 hours for emergency and relief purposes. Godsell recycled shipping containers to form the main volume of the building. The shack's parasol roof packs inside the container for shipping and when erected shades the container, reducing the building's heat load. The roof panels can also be interchanged with indigenous materials such as thatch, mud and stick, palm leaves and so on. Legs telescope from the container enabling it to be situated easily and without excavation on uneven terrain. The house has a variety of applications following flood, fire, earthquake or similar natural disasters, or functioning as temporary or relief lodgings.

Future Shack offers extreme flexibility since as a universal base module, containers can be stockpiled for use on an as-required basis and then transported by trucks, ships and trains worldwide. Easy to assemble on difficult sites, the shack comes packed with a pair of steel brackets, containing four legs that are fixed to the outside of the container. The units are admirably self-sufficient, arriving with water tanks, solar power cell, satellite receiver, roof access ladder, container access ramp and parasol roof, all stored inside the container during shipping. The basic container is also modified to provide thermal insulation and to allow the free flow of fresh air through a series of vents.

01
The Shack ships to its site packed with its components, including a parasol roof that reduces its heat load.
02, 03
Interior with kitchen and bathroom door panels open (top) and closed (bottom) with beds that fold down from the walls.
04
Longitudinal and cross section.
05
Roof elevation and floor plan.
06 [page 103]
Steel brackets and feet make the building easy to assemble, even on difficult terrain.

DESIGN HOSTEL

HOLZER KOBLER
ARCHITEKTUREN

Project location   Warnemünde, Germany
Estimated use   Hospitality
Container type   Freight container

01

01
The containers are stacked
four high atop a glass and
steel base.
02
Exterior passages leading
to the hostel rooms.
03
Double and dormitory-style
rooms are housed inside
the containers.
04
The cafe and workspace
on ground level.

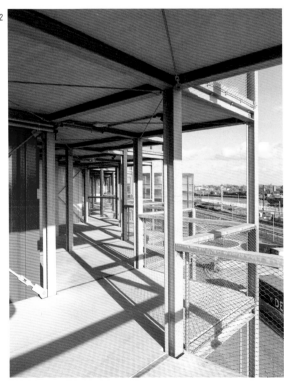

02

Situated in a port city in northern Germany, 76 shipping containers stacked along the harbor welcome hundreds of travelers looking for a night's rest. The design is constructed from intermodal containers, creating a visual link between the hostel and the city's shipping and shipbuilding tradition. The recycled, soundproof containers are brightly colored and stacked four stories high, echoing the formation of containers filled with consumer goods ready for transport. These sit atop a two-story steel, concrete, and glass structure that houses a light-filled entrance hall, where guests can mingle at the restaurant, bar, workspaces, and communal kitchen. Other amenities include a bouldering hall and a rooftop sauna and spa. The structure's playful link with the region's shipping tradition turned heads internationally, and landed the Zurich- and Berlin-based practice an Architecture MasterPrize 2019 in Hospitality Architecture. The jury lauded the space's atmosphere, and its ability to make "every holiday a truly unique experience".

INFINISKI MANIFESTO HOUSE

Architect

JAMES & MAU ARCHITECTS

Project location	Curacavi, Chile
Estimated use	Private residence
Container type	Freight container

01-03
For Infiniski James&Mau
repurposed mobile pallets to
dress their highly graphical
Manifesto House.

05

Infiniski, a green architecture and design company based in Spain and Chile have built a reputation on houses constructed from recycled shipping containers, pallets and train rails, even going so far as to design a large Chilean office building using salvaged shipping containers. James & Mau Architects' 160-square-meter (1,722-square-foot) Manifesto House for Infiniski is intended to represent the brand's concept, as well as its potential in terms of biocli-matic design, recycled and reused materials, nonpolluting construction systems, and the well-considered integration of renewable energy. Rescued maritime containers form the basis of the project, which relies on bioclimatic architecture to adapt the form and positioning of the house to its energy consumption and is based on a prefabricated, modular design that makes its construction both cheaper and faster. James & Mau divided the house into two levels, cutting a single container in half. The first story is used to support the container on the second level. This bridge-like approach to the structure generated a void between the staggered containers, which the architects isolated with thermo glass panels in order to provide a natural ventilation system. Also, as if it had a second skin, the house "dresses and undresses itself", the architects explain, depending on its need for solar heating, thanks to ventilated external solar panels that clad the walls and roof. The house's "skin" consists of sustainably harvested wooden panels on one side and recycled mobile pallets on the other. The pallets can open themselves in winter, allowing the sun to warm the metal surfaces of the containers, and close themselves in summer to protect the house from overheating. Both the exterior and the interior of Manifesto use up to 85% recycled, reused, and eco-friendly materials, including recycled cellulose and cork for insulation, recycled aluminum, iron, and wood and ecological paints.

04, 05
Interior views with exterior
wood panels open, leaving
large windows unshaded.
06
Wooden panels camouflage
rescued maritime containers
in the rear while pallets
clad the front of the house.
07
The residence uses up to 85%
recycled and green materials
inside and out.

07

HOMEBOXEN

HAN SLAWIK / ARCHITECH

Project location	Almere-Poort, Netherlands
Estimated use	Micro-residential house
Container type	Custom made six-meter wooden container

01

The project HomeBoxen is a continuation of HomeBox1. It represents an alternative to the standardized 6-meter ISO steel freight container: The proposed container is configured from thick timber walls with standard ISO corners, which means it can be easily shipped around the world. Realized as competition success in "Tiny Housing" in Almere, near Amsterdam, it explores the possibility of living in a container. Photovoltaic panels on the flat roofs provide the electrical power for hot water and heating. The homes are created from boxes in three different materials and dimensions: the six-meter timber container, the MicroBox add-on, which is a 2.44-meter wooden frame that functions as a winter garden, and the 1.8-meter MicroBox, a two-meter steel container that serves as a storage room. The vibrant primary colors blue, red and yellow of the containers are an intentional contrast to the drab grays and rusty reds of the surrounding buildings. By stacking the containers vertically, the individual units reduce their overall footprint. On the ground floor are the sanitary room, storage room, the kitchenette, the dining area and the access to the MicroBox. The middle level contains the sleeping area; the living area is on the highest level to benefit from the natural light and to have the best view. All boxes are transportable and can be differently configured elsewhere. The base was made with temporary steel screw piles.

01
HomeBoxen housing prototype installed in the Netherlands.
02
Vertically stacked containers minimize the overall footprint.
03
Internal staircase in a vertically stacked container.
04
The MicroBox acts as a winter garden, offers additional living space.
05
Technical sketches show views and sections with the different levels.

02

03

04

05

CASA ORUGA

SEBASTIAN IRARRAZAVAL

Project location	Lo Barnechea, Chile
Estimated use	Residential
Container type	Freight container

01

03

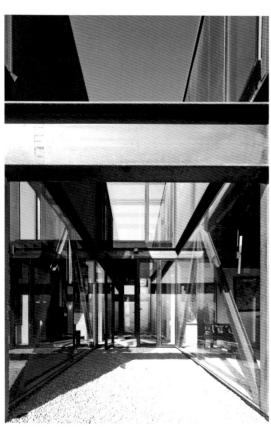

02

01
The downhill-facing facade.
02
The entrance.
03
The form of the building
sloping down the hill.
04
Swimming pool jacuzzi atop
the roof terrace.

04

Five standard 12-meter containers and six six-meter containers trace the gentle curve of a hill just outside Santiago, peeking out at the views on either side. There is an 11th container, too, its top removed for use as a swimming pool. The 350 square meter (3,767 square foot) home was built for an art collector and his family in a new suburb of the Chilean capital. The structure's adhesion to the hill was an important detail: in this region, the Andes are a strong visual and tectonic presence. The sloping form integrates the home into its mountainous surroundings. The ribboning volumes allow both light and alpine air to enter from either end, and to run smoothly and easily through the building—a key consideration to avoid mechanical cooling. Elements such as windows, doors, and skylights are rationalized and repeated throughout the house as both a cost-saving measure and to create a sense of harmony. The architect's rationale for the material selection was to mitigate cost, as well as ongoing maintenance efforts. Each material was selected for how well it ages, with the intention of adding value to the materiality and identity of the house over time.

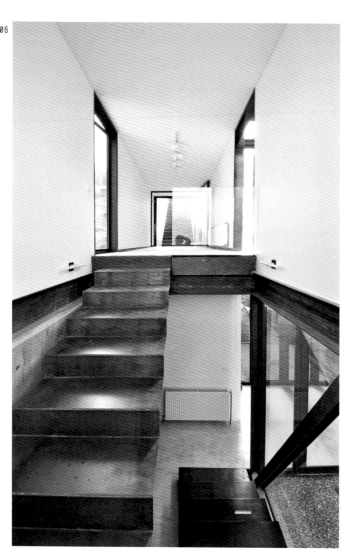

05, 06, 07
The light-filled interior.
08
The kitchen, opening onto
mountain views.

WIJN OF WATER

BIJVOET ARCHITECTUUR & STADSONTWERP

Project location   Rotterdam, the Netherlands
Estimated use   Restaurant
Container type   Freight container

01

02

03

04

01
Bijvoet salvaged nine freight containers from the nearby port to make this Mediterranean restaurant distinct.

02–04
Eight containers were lain horizontally; one, stacked vertically, becomes a tower that advertises the 50-seat venue and forms a small courtyard.

05, 06
Container doors become window shades and openings for generous views of the Maas River and port.

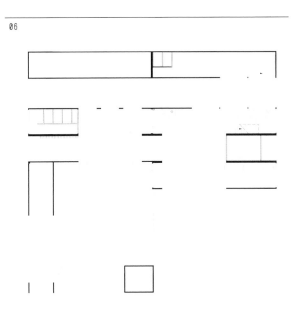

Dutch architect Caroline Bijvoet designed the temporary Wijn of Water restaurant in Rotterdam port. The exclusive Mediterranean cuisine and seating for 50 guests was targeted at the multicultural, creative and highly educated residents of the adjacent neighborhood. Views of the port and Maas River, along with a small budget and short construction timeline pointed towards using maritime elements in the architecture. Bijvoet used nine second-hand, 40-foot freight containers, eight of which she painted in a uniform light blue and stacked in two stories, arranged in an L-shape to form a southeast-facing atrium that is enclosed on three sides. The ninth container stands vertically, advertising the eatery. The position and shape of the building emphasizes the contrast between the built-up city to the north and the open, industrial views to the south, while providing protection against the prevailing westerly winds. To make the best use of the confined height of the containers, all equipment was installed in metal tubes on top of the roof of the building and full surface glazing was applied at the ends of the containers to allow light inside.

CHILDREN'S ACTIVITY CENTRE

Architect

PHOOEY ARCHITECTS

Project location	Melbourne, Australia
Estimated use	Adventure playground
Container type	Freight container

01, 03
Construction waste generated by slicing the recycled containers was reused for awnings and balustrades.
02
A tiled corridor. Phooey recycled 90% of its materials from site demolition and local sources.
04, 05
Containers were arranged to create both public and more intimate play areas, as well as to connect visually and physically with the surrounding landscape, a potential playground in itself.

01

02

03

The Children's Activity Centre is located at Skinner's Playground, behind a housing block in South Melbourne. Using the playful name "Phooey Architects", the theme of play is celebrated in this space through function, materiality and aesthetics. The brief was to produce a low-budget recreation centre with after-school facilities that could stand up to hyperactive kids—and to consult the community during the design process by initiating a local workshop around the project. The children themselves requested a two-story cub house with distinct spaces for boys and girls. In addition to these suggestions, Phooey decided to aim for zero waste, reusing containers that they assembled in a staggered arrangement that established both intimate and public spaces suitable for study, painting, dancing, and lounging. Each container was oriented strategically to produce visual and physical connections to surrounding playground areas. The architects turned the construction waste produced by slicing containers into a design feature, using the material for structural balustrade, awnings, and decorative cladding. This architectural approach translates the sustainable concept of feeding back into the building's lifecycle. Cannibalised and repositioned super-scale graphics give new life and character to the shipping containers while a timber deck, staircase, overhangs, awnings and bulk insulation shade the building and reduce energy use. Phooey also salvaged 90% of the materials used—including doors, windows, joinery, carpet tiles, timber, steel, and hardware—from site demolition, local council facilities and recyclers.

06

07

06
Both floors overhang a
small stream on the site.
07, 09
Pirated and repositioned
type and graphics add
another layer of whimsy
to the recreation centre.
08
A cross section of the
two-story building.

08

09

PLATOON CULTURAL DEVELOPMENT BERLIN

Architect

PLATOON.BERLIN & SOEREN ROEHRS

Project location   Berlin, Germany
Estimated use   Communication platform and office space
Container type   Freight container

01

02

03

01–03
The creative agency paired stacked freight containers with a matching patch of lawn and lap pool around which to host office parties and cultural events.
04
Site plan.

Founded in 2000, the Berlin offices of this multidisciplinary creative organization—whose projects focus on reality rather than the typical consumer wish to escape from it—are made, aptly enough, from freight containers. The 110-square-meter (1,184-square-foot) "communication platform" and office was made from four freight containers with the addition of a suitably railroad-track-shaped swimming pool. The containers are framed with plywood inside and planked with aluminum. One thing is made clear by this real-world industrial presentation of the company headquarters: "PLATOON does not entertain. PLATOON communicates." They just have a pool deck to do it on.

04

05
Platoon's offices was
one of their best bits
of branding yet.
06
The site of the Platoon
headquarters in Berlin.
07
Capping the ends of the
containers with glass fills
each floor with natural light.

07

Project

CONTAINER HOUSE (KILLER HOUSE)

Architect

ROSS STEVENS

Project location   Wellington, New Zealand
Estimated use   Private residence
Container type   Freight container

01

02

03

04

05

01
Stevens built this three-story part-time residence from pre-insulated containers and tower crane sections beside the local dump.
02
The bedroom.
03
Salvaged fire escape stairs and scrap steel fixtures and finishes.
04
Detail of the spiral staircase.
05
Clad in grey, the house exploits its site's geological flaws.
06, 07
The building leans into the embrace of three rock walls.

Stevens just wanted "a small basic place to sleep" when he had to work in the city, away from his rural home. Pursuing an ecologically and economically sustainable design while responding to the geological flaws of the site, inspired the architect to re-use refrigerated (pre-insulated) containers, tower crane sections, fire escape stairs, and pieces of industrial waste steel, all neatly assembled on the site of an abandoned hole in an excavated rock near the local rubbish dump. The building was designed to fit snugly into a space between three rock walls that give the dwelling shelter from wind and security when it is unoccupied. This idea led Stevens to limit the number of windows on the front of the building; instead he opted for 20 optical lenses that allow views out but not back in. Once inside, the rock becomes part of the building interior, allowing the house to feel both subterranean and open. Because the rock is not entirely stable, occasionally falling onto veranda floor, the designer forged the floor from 50-millimeter-thick industrial waste steel selected precisely to endure the impact. Incredibly, the site is also located on an active earthquake fault line that is expected to cause serious damage to the city in the next 50 years (a fact of which the fractured and falling rock serves as a constant visual reminder) further justifying Stevens' use of industrial products in the construction of a strong yet lightweight shelter.

06

07

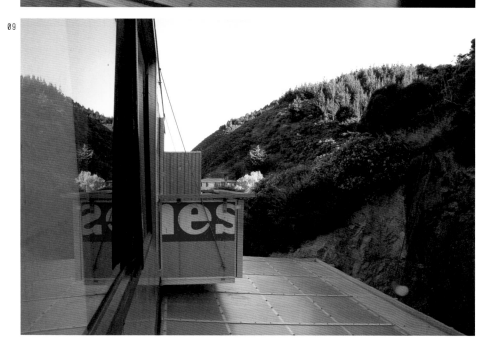

08, 09
Cargo numbers and caution signs allude to the former functions of Stevens' construction components.
10, 11
Floor plans.
12
Scrap metal and the living rock wall that buttresses the house are decorative elements in the design.
13
The industrial salvaging means that the interior sometimes recalls an old-fashioned train carriage.

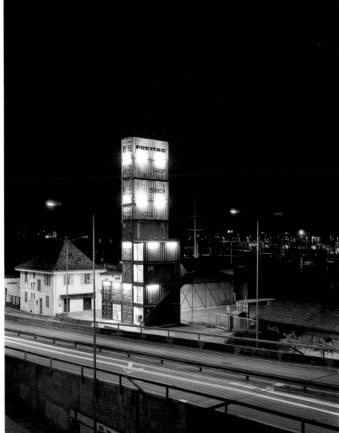

01

FREITAG FLAGSHIP STORE ZURICH

Architect

SPILLMANN ECHSLE ARCHITEKTEN

Project location	Zurich, Switzerland
Estimated use	Retail space and observation platform
Container type	Freight container

04

01
Located on a regional transport hub, Freitag's Zurich flagship is a tower of freight containers that echoes the brand's ecofriendly ethos.

02, 03
Interior views of retail and showroom space.

04
Spillmann Echsle stacked 17 containers, fixing them in place with shipping industry fasteners.

05
An observation platform tops the showrooms 25 meters above the Geroldstrasse neighborhood.

As much landmark as showroom, the 120-square-meter (1,292-square-foot) Zurich Freitag Flagship Store comes crowned—and crowns the city—with an observation platform. The architecture represents an extension of the brand's recycling ethos: since 1993, Freitag has manufactured bags made from repurposed truck tarpaulins, an idea inspired by the company's view of the nearby bridge. Spillmann Echsle architects found 17 freight containers in Hamburg and of course, shipped them to Zurich by rail. They then stacked the colorful boxes (fixing them with shipping industry fasteners) low enough so as to not violate the city's restriction on high-rise construction in the surrounding Geroldstrasse neighborhood, in which the shop is located. The area has long been shaped by its location at the center of several transportation lines (including both rail and auto) and its industrial fabric: a low-slung, smattering of buildings and highly trafficked storage infrastructure. The retail space is situated at the base of the stack, while the tower contains showrooms. Generous window openings saturate the interiors with natural light and allow views in both directions, from the inside out and the outside in. Shoppers circulate past the full product range, which includes more than 150 bags, and then ascend to the observation platform 25 meters above ground with a view of the city, the ribbons of traffic, and Zurich's picturesque alpine lake. The design preserves the same view onto the bridge that gave birth to the Freitag bag concept in the first place.

Project
JOSHUA TREE RESIDENCE
Architect
WHITAKER STUDIO

Project location   Joshua Tree, USA
Estimated use   Residential
Container type   Freight container

01

02

01, 03
Interior renders showing
bedrooms branching out
from the entrance hall.
02, 04
Exterior renders showing the
home against the dramatic
Californian landscape.

03

Joshua Tree Residence, which is planned for completion in 2020, almost did not happen. The structure was originally conceptualized 10 years prior for an advertising agency in Germany, which backed out before construction began. A private client in Los Angeles asked Whitaker Studio if the idea could be revisited as a holiday home on a striking plot of land in the Mojave Desert, outside the small town of Joshua Tree. This region of southern California has long been fertile ground for architectural experimentation, from Andrea Zittel's sleeping pods to Albert Frey's modernist residences in nearby Palm Springs. For the architecture studio, the new site was a perfect match. The structure is inspired by the growth of crystals in a laboratory, and the effect is achieved through 19 white shipping containers welded together on site. The placement of each of these is defined by the surrounding landscape: the kitchen is oriented to catch the morning sun, while more private spaces like the en-suite bathrooms face a rocky slope. The composition was designed with a dramatic entrance in mind. According to the architects, when all internal doors are open, you can stand in the middle and look out at the radiating spokes on all sides.

05, 06
Each bedroom is positioned
in its own container.
07
The containers that point
skywards fill the home with
natural light.
08
The architects referred to
Joshua Tree as "the perfect
match" for this particular
building form.

LIVE/WORK SPACE

SCULP(IT) ARCHITECTEN

Project location   Antwerp, Belgium
Estimated use   Private residence and office space
Container type   Container look

01

02

03

01
On a tiny 2.4-meter-wide Antwerp lot, the entire storefont of this architecture office swings open to serve as its door.
02
The living room on the second floor.
03
Kitchen and dining room look out from the first floor.
04
Each wooden floor was inserted shelf-life into a frame set between th existing walls of this remnant city parcel and is lit with a unique colour at night.

In Antwerp's red light district, not all the lights are red. Architects Pieter Peerlings and Silvia Mertens of Sculp(It) live and work in a remnant space that is a mere 2.4 meters wide, 5.5 meters deep and 12 meters high and have created a light installation out of their home. Each of the four wooden floors, which were inserted between two existing walls and slotted into a steel frame, take on their own hue at night. The ground floor serves as the architects' studio and is illuminated in white, the kitchen/dining room on the first floor is green, the living room on the second floor glows red, while the third-floor bedroom is lit blue. The building's shelf-like floors are connected by a spiral staircase that was tucked into the space in a single piece. Three black polyethylene tubes, arranged vertically and horizontally and housed between double wooden floors, provide the infrastructure for plumbing, heating and electricity. Outfitted with a porcelain bathtub, the roof is dedicated to (sun)bathing. The street-level office is fitted with a glassy storefront which is also a door that is as wide as the site. In fact, the designers glazed the whole facade with large, black-framed panes that give a nod (and perhaps a wink, too) to the professionals who formerly occupied this neighborhood—the prostitutes.

CONTAINR
CINEMA

ROBERT DUKE
ARCHITECT

WITH KIETH DOYLE, IAIN SINCLAIR, NICOLE MION AND EVANN SIEBENS

Project location	Vancouver, British Colombia, Canada
Estimated use	Event space
Container type	Freight container

04

01

02

03

01, 02
A pop-up theatre and sustainable architecture.
03
A number of Vancouver artists contributed to the development of this cultural container-in-a-container.
04
The boxes were stacked, staggered and painted.
05
Inside, surfaces were cut away to create a double-height ceiling.

In Vancouver's Public Library Square, a consortium of local artists under the direction of architect Robert Duke, developed containR as a temporary way to bring art and ideas directly into the public realm. The project combined video, public art and sustainable urban design. As a branded object, it is a modular portable event space that can be dropped into place and assembled within several hours. containR is a pair of unevenly stacked freight containers that have been cut away to create a double-height interior, with a projector and screen tucked into opposite ends of the vaulted void of the upper container. The upper container is cantilevered beyond the lower one by 10 feet, defining a dramatic exit and entrance while solar panels have been integrated into the architecture, doubling as an aesthetic element. From the outside, passers by during the city's 2009 Cultural Olympiad viewed graphic painting and watched a video monitor that screened a documentary about the object's construction. In the future, the multipurpose box will also be programmed for use as a gallery, retail outlet, DJ/VJ club, live stage and possibly even low-cost housing, says Duke.

05

Project
QIYUN MOUNTAIN CAMP
Architect
LOT-EK

Project location   Qiyun Mountain, China
Estimated use   Sports park
Container type   Freight container

01

02

03

01
The camp seen in context with its natural surroundings.
02, 03
The site is color-coded based on function.
04
Containers on an angle allow visitors to explore the landscape from different vantage points.
05
Aerial view.

More than pristine landscapes, China's Qiyun Mountain is one of the four sacred mountains of Taoism and believed to be the place of origin of the yin-yang symbol. Situated amid the verdant peaks, Qiyun Mountain Camp is an adventure and extreme sports park—the largest of its kind in China. The base units are made from shipping containers cut on a bias, which are joined, mirrored, and tilted together forming a dynamic set of structures. The clusters zigzag, project on a diagonal axis and, at the focal point of the park, emanate outwards in a star-shaped volume. The sprawling complex is divided up into several different clusters, each color-coded to help orientate guests. It contains shops, cafes, service areas, pergolas, and observation decks to take in the landscapes. In the yellow and blue area, a restaurant plaza is situated on a hill overlooking the river below and forming an outdoor amphitheater. Another container, hoisted up in a diagonal, is a launch platform for a zip line. Near the lake, a cluster of modular units forms changing areas, cafes, and storage for kayaks. The buildings encourage flow towards the lake, where a floating pier stretches into the water.

Project
ORBINO
Architect
LUC DELEU

Project location   Amsterdam-West, Noordzeekanaal, Netherlands
Estimated use   Sculpture and observation platform
Container type   Freight container

01

02

Orbino is a permanent, 45-square-meter (485-square-foot) open-air sculpture on the Noordzeekanaal in Amsterdam. Belgian architect and artist Luc Deleu's walk-through art work is made from three rehabilitated shipping containers with screw bridge fittings, stacking cones, a steel staircase, and a concrete base. It plays with the relationship between horizontal and vertical. Deleu arranged the containers in a precarious pile: the L-shaped tower resembles a periscope because the upper containers cantilever out over empty air by two container-widths. A steel staircase mounted to the exterior leads to a room formed by the three highest containers, two-thirds of which consists of the cantilevered box. With floor-to-ceiling glazing on one side, this interior acts as an enclosed observation platform.

01, 03, 04
A periscope-like cantilevering of containers serves as artwork and vista in Antwerp.
02
Orbino seen in elevation drawings.
05
The observation platform is accessed via a staircase anchored to the rear of the tower.

Project
BIENNALE OF INDEPENDENT SPACES FOR ART
Architect
BUREAU A

Project location	Geneva, Switzerland
Estimated use	Temporary event space
Container type	Freight container

01

03

02

01
The boxes were stacked on
both sides and ends to create
a variety of interiors.
02
Not just fine art exhibition
spaces, the containers supported a variety of events.
03
The circle of 48 containers
formed a steel Stonehenge and
a democratic cultural milieu.

Swiss architecture firm Bureau A playfully mimics one of the wonders of the world with Steelhenge, a cluster of 50 disused shipping containers arranged in a circular formation. Not quite as mysterious in construction as its English counterpart, the cluster of containers were brought in to create a weekend-long open air venue in Genevas, as part of the first biennale for independent art spaces in Geneva. To the architects, Stonehenge was a particularly interesting reference for the pagan rituals it is associated with—which, in turn, the architects associated with Geneva's alternative and squat culture in Geneva. The container itself—readily available and easily reused—was a viable choice given the restricted budget and that the pavilion would only be in use for a long weekend. The structure in its entirety was built within a single day with the help of a crane and concrete blocks to stabilize the containers. Painted blue and ranged in a radiant circle, the containers established a striking contrast with the chalky red dirt floor of the public plaza.

PLATOON KUNSTHALLE SEOUL

Architect

PLATOON AND GRAFT ARCHITECTS

WITH U-IL ARCHITECTS

Project location   Seoul, Korea
Estimated use   Event space
Container type   Freight container

In the upscale Cheongdam area, beside upscale galleries and boutiques, PLATOON KUNSTHALLE Seoul's 950-square-meter (10,225-square-foot) space for events, exhibitions, art studios, a workshop, a public library, offices, and a bar and restaurant, consists of 28 reinforced cargo containers that have been stacked and welded together. Graft Architects' framed, plasterboard, mineral wool and aluminium plate interiors are dedicated to hosting art and cultural events, shows and workshops that usually fall beneath the radar, including street art, graphic design, fashion, video art, programming, music, club culture, and political activism. The salvaged containers express this alternative institutional character in a dynamic space made from what have become icons of flexible, responsible architecture in today's "Think Global, Act Local" atmosphere. They can also be rebuilt anywhere, at any time. This is no small virtue.

01

01
Floor plans.
02, 03
Views of the rear
of the building.
04
Front facade of
the event space.

05

05
The building in sections.
06
The glazed ends of containers
are juxtaposed with the
windowless longitudinal sides
of adjacent containers.

07, 10
The main hall.
08
The library.
09
An industrial gate serves
as a side door and window.

Project
EICHBAUMOPER
Architect
RAUMLABORBERLIN
JAN LIESEGANG AND MATTHIAS RICK

Project location   Mülheim an der Ruhr, Germany
Estimated use   Event space
Container type   Freight container

01

02

Through four humble shipping containers, raumlaborberlin architects Jan Liesegang and Matthias Rick transformed a problematic underground station that had long suffered from vandalism and violent assaults into a 50-square-meter (538-square-foot) opera house. The project represented a communal effort to rehabilitate a beleaguered public space through architecture, art and theater. The three-story space contained an office and workshop, stage, a room for community meetings and a "laboratory." With Liesegang and Rick as artistic directors, the container frame system, with partial steel-structure reinforcements, stood for one year. Inside, a new type of opera was created in an unusual collaboration between designers, musicians, artists and local people. Part of the libretto was taken directly from resident's stories of waiting at the station and when the performances began in mid-2009, 60 residents participated as extras. Normal train service was maintained during show times, and some even took place inside the trains en route between Essen and the Hirschlandplatz stop in Mülheim.

04

05

06

07

01
The container-based cultural
space gave new life to a
crime-ridden rail station.
02
The project seen in section.
03
The space closed up.
04
Interior office space.
05
The space open to the public.
06
Exterior view.
07
Site plan showing the unusual
arrangement of volumes.

DEVIL'S CORNER CELLAR DOOR

Architect

CUMULUS STUDIO

Project location	Apslawn, Australia
Estimated use	Commercial and hospitality
Container type	Freight container

01

03

Despite its name, Devil's Corner Cellar Door, Lookout & Market is situated on a heavenly part of the Tasmanian east coast, amidst one of the island's largest vineyards. Previously, the building was a single demountable structure, which Australian practice Cumulus Studio expanded to include the lookout and space for culinary experiences and events. The design aimed to boost the winery's profile with an additional experiential layer, creating for its visitors a wine-tasting experience with panoramic views of the Freycinet Peninsula. The structure, built from anthracite gray and timber-clad containers, plays with the idea that wine can be appreciated in many "in-mouth" sensations. The architects have applied this notion to the building itself, creating a series of views that allow the visitor to explore the landscape through different vantage points. The floorplan is divided into three distinct spaces: sky, horizon, and tower, each designated to reference the different views of the site.

02

01
The Cellar Door market
surrounds a courtyard space.
02
The open deck overlooking
the vineyards.
03
The vertically stacked
container forms the
lookout, a visual signifier
of the design.
04
Southern elevation
of the lookout.

1   lookout southern elevation
1:100

05
The lookout offers several
vantage points for visitors to
take in different perspectives
of the landscape.
06
A horizontal view
corridor carved out of
the container's side.
07
Visitors climb the stairs
towards the topmost viewpoint.
08
The visitors' experience is
designed as a loose collection
of containers.

08

CONSTRUCTION X, HOORN BRIDGE, SPEYBANK

Architect

LUC DELEU

Project location	Antwerp, Belgium (Construction X and Speybank)
	Hoorn, the Netherlands (Hoorn Bridge)
Estimated use	Scuptures and bridge
Container type	Freight container

01

02

03

01
Construction X.
02
The Hoorn Bridge.
03
Speybank.

Over the past two decades, Belgian artist Luc Deleu has created sculptural and architecturally oriented pieces by integrating industrial containers into his work in forms that range from A to Z. Made for the 1990 exhibition For Real Now, Construction X on the Hoorn Bridge in the Netherlands worked triple time as an artwork and a 30-square-meter (323-square-foot) pedestrian and bicycle bridge. Deleu removed the rear walls of two 20-foot containers and, as he is wont to do, used screw bridge fittings and special interconnecting devices to fix the containers in place. The Speybank sculpture resembled a bridge, with four impossibly balanced containers forming a vast horseshoe that seems ready to collapse at any moment. Construction X, on the other hand, was a less functional, albeit more stable looking, construction.

Project

CONSUMER TEMPLE – BROKEN ICON

Architect

GARY DEIRMENDJIAN

Project location   Sydney, NSW, Australia
Estimated use   Sculpture
Container type   Freight container

01
The view upward into the artwork.
02
Looking down to the pallet floor and "buttresses".
03
Deirmendjian cut openings into one wall of the container to create a church-like dimness.

The work sits in the green expanse, a singular presence in a state of stable decay. A narrow entrance leads into an intimately walled enclosure which offers no way out other than that of entry. Only fragments of the outer world are discernible through the walls. In the relative darkness, the eye is drawn up to the airy chamber high above, where light beams through small windows onto a centrally suspended, broken cash register. The container is held upright with its opening facing down, atop four stacks of timber pallets. A combination of ground anchors, cables and tensioning secure the structure to the ground. An enclosure is created by walling off the three sides of the four pallet stacks, using a variety of pallets and commercial crates—a combination that also allows for seating. Small rectangular apertures cut into the container's timber floor, allow limited light in.

PUMA CITY
LOT-EK

Project location   Alicante, Spain
                    Boston, Massachusetts, USA
Estimated use   Retail and event space
Container type   Freight container

01

01, 03
The fragmented logo, pulled
apart by shifting the stack
of containers, advertised the
architecture as much as Puma
City, itself.
02
Fully glazed ends of the
containers let in light and
framed views to the interior.
03
The stack shift created
double-height ceilings on the
lower floors and open spaces
that let in light, air and
circulation routes.
04
Two retail spaces filled the
lower levels with offices and
storage on the first floor and
a terrace and event space at
the top.
05, 06
Section drawings.

Taking full advantage of the global shipping network already in place, New York studio LOT-EK retrofitted 24 cargo containers to transform them into Puma City. Puma City was a movable 1,020-square-meter (10,980-square-foot) retail and event space that, along with the 70-foot long Puma sailing boat, il mostro, toured the world during a year-long marketing campaign for the athletic gear retailer. Like the sailboat, the City was fully demountable and traveled on a cargo ship. Ada Tolla and Giovanni Lignano conceived of the building as a three-story stack of containers, staggered to create internal outdoor spaces, large overhangs and terraces. The stack was then branded with the super-graphic logo of the company which appeared

intriguingly fragmented as a result of the stack shift. Puma City featured two full retail spaces on the lower levels, both with large double-height ceilings, as well as with four-container-wide open spaces to challenge the modular boxy quality of the containers' interiors. The second level was occupied by offices, a press area and storage while on the top floor, a bar, lounge and event space opened out onto a large terrace. The construction used 40-foot shipping containers as well as a number of the existing container connectors to join and secure the units both horizontally and vertically. Each module was designed to ship as a conventional cargo container through a system of structural covering panels that fully sealed all

of its large openings. These seals were then removed on site to reconnect the large, open interiors. With this project, LOT-EK challenged the scale at which a building could be truly mobile, and designed Puma City to confront all of the architectural obstacles faced by a building of its kind, including international building codes, dramatic climate changes, plug-in electrical and HVAC systems and ease of constant assembly, disassembly and operations.

05

06

07, 08
Shop interiors on the lower floors.
09
By removing container walls, LOT-EK created high ceilings and greater transparency.
10
An entry arcade created at ground level by the first floor containers.

Project
COMMON GROUND
Architect
URBANTAINER
AND OFFICE 53427

Project location   Seoul, South Korea
Estimated use   Commercial
Container type   Freight container

01

02

Before Common Ground was built, the site was an underutilized piece of land in the middle of Seoul. Within half a year of completion, it was a bustling shopping center, designed to create connections between people and the first of its kind in South Korea to be built entirely from shipping containers. The 200 containers that make up the structure were prepared in a factory off-site and transported to the lot for assembly.

This helped reduce the construction phase for the 5,300 square meter (57,049 square foot) shopping mall to just five months. The structure's form is dictated by its relatively narrow plot of land, connecting two main volumes with a public square in-between. One building's interior echoes a market hall, where vertically stacked container frames are used to articulate the space, while the other side, echoing a street market, retains the industrial feeling of the containers where possible. Interior elements, like hanging planters, mimic the form of the shipping containers throughout. At street level, compositions of the containers are formulated to create intrigue and attract foot traffic. Everything about Common Ground was created to forge meaningful interaction and connections between people. The graphic identity, shown across the building's facade, echoes the form of the shipping containers, while conveying a sense of coming together.

01, 02, 03
The containers are staggered along the facade to invite passersby.
04
Overlooking the retail environment.
05
Dining along the terrace.

05

06
The facade.
07, 08
The space is inspired by
the market and conveys
a sense of coming together.
09
Common Ground against
the wider urban context.

09

SUBURBAN HOUSE KIT

Architect

ADAM KALKIN

Project location   New York City, New York, USA
Estimated use   Installation
Container type   Freight container

01

03

04

02

01
Scenography for the Deitch Gallery exhibition re-created a fantasy suburbia in which a residence comes ready-made in a freight container.
02, 04
Interiors that articulated the wastefulness of suburban living alongside responsible design.
03
The container house kit wouldn't have been complete without the car parked in the driveway.

Dipping into your midlife crisis? It may be time to acquire a new life-in-a-box. The Suburban House Kit is a suburban idyll conceived by Adam Kalkin with artists and designers including Tobias Rehberger and shown at Manhattan's Deitch Projects gallery as an artwork. In addition to a fully equipped and furnished home assembled from freight containers, the house came with an origami garden, a courtyard, a car and garage, and other amenities typical of the suburban American way of life. Best of all, it can be ordered as a complete architectural and lifestyle "kit". The use of freight containers in this cheeky project—which was simultaneously critical and optimistic—set its ironic tone since it juxtaposed unconventional building materials with the supremely conventional design features of suburbia; wastefulness with responsible living.

OLD LADY HOUSE

ADAM KALKIN

Project location   Califon, New Jersey, USA
Estimated use   Private residence
Container type   Freight container

01

New Jersey-based architect Adam Kalkin created this 93-square-meter (1,000-square-foot) house from freight containers and a large, wrap-around deck. Its simple and energy-efficient, single-story plan was designed to enable an elderly person to be able to live alone and enjoy an easily maintained domestic space. The central box features automatic glass doors at either end leading to the deck from the front and rear of the home and contains the dining and living zones. To one side of the main living room, another container holds the kitchen, laundry room, and a walk-in closet. Flanking the opposite side of the living room are two bedrooms and a bathroom. In some sections, the architect removed container walls, floors or ceilings to create double-height spaces. Due to its intelligent use of space-saving container modules, the house offers a number of spacious interior rooms that are easily accessible and maintainable.

01
This energy-efficient home can be easily maintained by its elderly owner, prolonging her independence into old age.

02
A wraparound porch gives easy
access to rooms up the slope.
03, 04
Interiors feature generous
glazing.
05
Two volumes flank
a cozy patio.
06
The patio connects ground
floor entrances.
07
The basic unit of the design.

12 CONTAINER HOUSE

ADAM KALKIN

Project location   Brooklin, Maine, USA
Estimated use   Private residence
Container type   Freight container

02

03

01

04

The 12 Container House, used as a summer and vacation house, was built on the rugged Atlantic coastline of Brooklin in Maine, outside the city and surrounded by trees. Its basic structure follows the principle of combining containers with other structural elements, in this case a prefabricated steel-glass construction forming the central living hall. The house consists of 12 salvaged freight containers that set on a common reinforced concrete slab, form the exterior walls of the central, two-story, roofed living space. They are grouped around the hall to form two T-shaped units. Two containers are stacked upon each other. The ground-floor containers along with the hall accommodate a spacious living, dining and kitchen space, while the upper containers serve as private bedrooms. Open stairs lead from the central living space to the upper story. The front walls of the containers are fully glazed, also toward the interior space, thus offering additional lighting from the hall. The long sides are all closed to the outside, but some are fully open to the inside to integrate the kitchen and dining room into the living room. The gabled sides of the living room can be opened by means of lowering industrial garage doors, thus making it a sort of buffer or intermediate space between the outdoors and the completely enclosed containers.

01
An isometric view
of the house.
02
Front facade.
03
Rear view with some
container walls
replaced by windows.
04
The north and
south elevations.
05
Looking through the
open industrial gate
to the dining room.
06
Kitchen.
07
Stair detail.

06

07

09

10

11

08
Twin staircases seem to wink
at the traditional grand stair
in this industrial, modern-day
"mansion."
09
The library niche.
10
Plan of the first floor.
11
Second floor plan.

Project
INCUBO HOUSE
Architect
MARIA JOSE TREJOS ARCHITECT

Project location   San Jose, Costa Rica
Estimated use   Private residence
Container type   High cube freight containers

01

02

01
A bamboo "skin" filters light
all around the house.
02
One roof boasts a lush
green lawn.
03
The containers cluster around
a double-height interior.
04
A tilted roof promotes air
flow through the building.

Eight high cube containers set into steel frames on concrete foundations form this family home, with a sturdy cedar tree growing majestically in the middle. The formation ensured the mature tree would not have to be cleared for the home, instead it creates a living focal point throughout the home. The containers meet in a central two-story space that serves as a cross-ventilation "lung." The bedrooms and private spaces are all organized on the second floor, connected via an exposed walkway that leads to a staircase, constructed from the cedar tree's branches, which in turn leads to the third-floor terrace. Bridging the four containers generated 95 square meters (1,022 square feet) of additional space, radically reducing the amount and cost of building materials. Beyond the repurposed containers, the home features several eco-friendly qualities, including a solar water heater, recycled plastic and wood decking, LED lighting and a foam aluminum insulation system. The living room floor is made from handsome concrete while the bedrooms feature bamboo underfoot. Bamboo was also used to create a light-filtering coating over the northeastern facade.

B-CAMP
HELEN & HARD
ARCHITEKTEN

Project location	Stavanger, Norway
Estimated use	Private residence and studio space
Container type	Building container

01

02

Norwegian architects Helen & Hard Architekten have worked on several recycling projects which reuse construction materials and components discarded by the oil industry. This experiment has been made easier by the studio's proximity to the site of the largest Norwegian oil reserves, where many international oil companies are located. B-Camp is situated on the coast at Stavanger, on a former industrial site, and involved the transformation of ten discarded industrial containers into four residential apartments, which are intended to serve as a type of "incubator" center for start-up companies and young, creative freelancers.

This low-budget dwelling alternative features tiny 25–35-square-meter (269–377-square-foot) units, whose diminutive square-footage is balanced with higher-than-usual ceilings, bi-level plans, and individual terraces on the upper levels. The repurposed container units, which were once used as accommodation on their original industrial site, were fitted with a jumble of irregularly framed but generous window openings and additional doors. The units are composed of surplus windows and doors, scrap materials from the metal industry, and clad with a transparent, corrugated plastic panels that have a thermally insulating effect, meaning

that only five centimeters of additional insulation was necessary in order to provide satisfactory heat-loss protection. B-Camp offers an alternative lifestyle option for young people who aspire to work in a creative environment and enjoy affordable housing with individual character. In addition, the Helen & Hard offices, which are located close by, also rent out office facilities which include seminar and conference rooms, and social and break areas to B-Camp residents.

01
B-Camp is located on a former industrial site close to Norways largest oil reserves and refineries.
02
The architects cut irregular window openings into industrial building containers to create apartments for young workers.

03

05

06

07

03, 07
Site plans and isometric
rendering showing the
beautiful disorder of the
containers' two stories.
04, 08
Views from outside.
05, 06
Small living spaces
are offset with high
rooms, bilevel plans
and lots of light.

08

Project
ARCHITEKTURBOX
Architect
SHE-ARCHITEKTEN

ULRICH HAHNEFELD, MARCO PAWLIK, STEPHEN PERRY, STEPHAN SCHRICK AND TORSTEN STERN

Project location   Hamburg, Germany
Estimated use   Event space and information center
Container type   Container frame

This information kiosk was designed to stand for six days during Hamburg's Architecture Summer event. In the city center and opposite the city's Gallery of Contemporary Art, the delightfully odd structure, with a cafe that sat astride a small terrace overlooking the water, served as an information center for the public, a promotional hub for events and destinations, and a rest stop for fair visitors. Architects Torsten Stern, Marco Pawlik, Stephen Perry, Stephan Schrick and Ulrich Hahnefeld envisioned the building as a pavilion for visitors to the city and the event, as well as a forum for exhibitions, lectures and discussions. The team decided to pile container frames instead of tidily stacking them, giving the structure textural intrigue against the skyline and city fabric.

The exterior of the container frames were clad with everything from metal, glass and wood to finishes of many hues. Potential architectural clients (including those who didn't realize they would become clients following the event, one assumes) were able to browse this library of building materials and finishes while they were in use. Inside, the center was also filled with information for professionals and non-professionals alike.

01–03
Floor plans and elevations detailing the layout of materials and finishes on the information kiosk interior and facade.
04, 07
The kiosk was a patchwork of architectural products and a pile instead of a neat stack of container frames of various volumes.
05, 06
The structure hosted a product library and a small terrace cafe overlooking the water.

02

01

03

05

06

07

BED BY NIGHT

HAN SLAWIK

Project location   Hanover, Germany
Estimated use   Social service centre
Container type   Building container / freight container

Slawik rehabilitated a single-story structure, assembled from 14 construction site containers, to provide temporary lodgings and social services for street children. As part of the conversion, which will be used for up to 10 years, existing containers were reused and additional modules added. The container ensemble, which Slawik dubbed a "container village", is housed in a protective and insulating premounted industrial glass shell. Slawik placed the new two-story, 361-square-meter (3,886-square-foot) space on a frost-proof foundation made of large prefabricated concrete slabs, giving the wooden frame visible joints and attaching the glass facade via explicitly exposed fixtures, to ensure that all structural components were clearly visible. The architecture is meant to give the kids who use it a literal example of the term "support": the conspicuously jointed building serves as a metaphor for the social "loadbearing" that the street children are being taught inside its walls.

01, 02
Slawik painted building and freight containers in primary colors and arranged them in two stories.
03
The "container village" is visible inside an industrial glass shell.
04, 05
Floor plans for ground and first floors.
06, 08, 09
The glass shell is insulating and guards a front courtyard.
07
An exploded view of the containers within the wooden frame and glass shell.

06

08

07

09

Project

TRINITY BUOY WHARF (CONTAINER CITY I+II)

Architect

NICHOLAS LACEY AND PARTNERS

Project location   London, Great Britain
Estimated use   Housing and studio spaces
Container type   Freight container

01

01–04
The porthole-dotted facades of Lacey's Trinity Buoy Wharf housing with container doors folded down into balconies.
05
East elevation.
06
West elevation.
07
North elevation.

On the London Docklands, Nicholas Lacey and Partners used recycled freight containers to build colorful art studios and live-work apartments. Container Cities I and II are situated on Trinity Buoy Wharf, a peninsula at the eastern end of the Docklands. Part of the area's redevelopment into a cultural center for the arts, Buro Happold engineered the projects, which were built in two phases. Container City I was deployed in only three months from fifteen 40-foot containers that were stacked three-high to create 12 workshops, while Container City II added 30 more. The two structures are serviced by a common vertical circulation core and connected by bridges. Two types of windows were used: a large pivoting porthole and a sliding glass door that replaced the standard double doors at the end of each box. Anchored in the open position, these doors now serve as a balcony. The team sprayed the interior of each container with insulation over membrane waterproofing and finished the walls and ceiling in plasterboard. Constructed from 80% recycled materials, the Cities enjoy a long waiting list for rental.

KEETWONEN
TEMPOHOUSING/
JMW ARCHITEKTEN

Project location   Amsterdam, the Netherlands
Estimated use   Student housing
Container type   Freight container

01–03
Scarlet framing gives the
1,000 student dormitories a
crisp sartorial appearance.
In clean rows, the apartments
stretch over 17,000 square
meters (182,986 square feet).
04
Mailboxes at one building's
entrance and the stairwell
that leads to each of the
five floors.
05–07
Construction photos show that
the distinctive red frames are
simply an articulation of the
red container walls that are
the bones of the buildings.

01

02

03

This project was situated in the southeast of Amsterdam, near the highway and a subway station, making it eminently accessible. On a plot of 17,000 square meters (182,986 square feet), Tempohousing and the De Key housing corporation built a small village of one thousand individual 30-square-meter student dormitories. The entire project consists of six blocks of buildings of varying sizes, arranged to create courtyards that can be used as bicycle parking and social space. The units are stacked up to five levels and sit beside an outdoor basketball field, a supermarket, a launderette, a café, a bicycle repair shop, and several office spaces, built in 34 40-foot containers. To access the living units, staircases and exterior walkways were constructed on the sides facing the courtyard. On the opposite side, each unit has a private balcony. With all its conveniences, the project is also designed to be completely mobile. After five years at this location, it will be transported to a new site in the Netherlands or beyond, since the constituent containers have a Container Safety Convention (CSC) plate and are considered standard freight on container vessels that sail around the globe. All of the living spaces were rented out early on in the project; subsequently the waiting list for rental has grown to over 1.5 years. Keetwonen, which was most likely the largest container village in existence at the time, won a Funda Award in 2006 for "Best executed innovation in construction".

05

06

07

RAINES COURT

ALLFORD HALL MONAGHAN MORRIS

Project location Stoke Newington, London, Great Britain
Estimated use Residential housing
Container type Building container

01

02

Raines Court is an £8.9 million building whose design and construction served as an investigation into the potential of off-site volumetric construction. Raines was also the first housing corporation-funded modular housing scheme in the UK. The client, the Peabody Trust, asked AHMM to create high quality flats for sale that would include 41 two-bedrooms, 11 three-bedrooms, one single bedroom, and eight live/work units over three separate blocks, all linked by a central circulation core. The architects had the dwellings manufactured as fully-fitted modules off-site, to factory standards, focusing on maximizing the size of the modules while minimizing the number of components being constructed off-site. The apartments incorporate a fire escape strategy developed in response to the module dimensions; they minimize circulation while maximizing useable area. South-facing covered balconies and private courts that branch off an open walkway are incorporated into the modules, which because they are well-insulated, have low energy requirements and a diminished cost in use. One interesting result of the prefab work undertaken was the record it produced, articulating a number of potential long-term benefits of modular construction including: diminished waste and increased recycling, the greater predictability of the construction process, reduced transportation and disruption of local environments, superior quality control and maintenance, reduced construction time, and increased safety, along with most simply—more cost-effective building. It is worth noting that the Raines Court flats were all sold within weeks of being put on the market.

03

04

05

06

01
Three blocks of prefabricated
flats are linked by a central
circulation core.
02
Balconies.
03
Because the units were manufactured off-site, the architects were able to maximise
their size while reducing the
number of components.
04
Apartment interior.
05
South-facing covered balconies.
06
Second floor plan.

Project
CANCER CENTER
AMSTERDAM
Architect
MVRDV

Project location   Amsterdam, the Netherlands
Estimated use   Hospital
Container type   Building container

01

02

01
MVRDV built vertically on the small site to create a temporary cancer clinic from container-like boxes.
02
The red and blue pixels of the facade emphasises the seemingly modular nature of the building.
03
Beside a major highway, the architecture becomes advertising for the hospital.

During the rebuilding and enlargement of this Amsterdam cancer research and treatment clinic, a part of the Antony van Leeuwenhoek Hospital, Rotterdam-based architects MVRDV designed a temporary institute that could be erected during the construction process. The architects envisioned the temporary structure as a series of containers stacked seven stories high, with a floor space of 1,425 square meters (15,339 square feet). Located on a small site next to the A19 motorway, it was obvious that the project required a vertical architectural solution. The designers viewed the clinic's location beside one of the country's busiest highways as an opportunity instead of an obstacle. To make the Cancer Center more high profile, they painted each container in various shades of blue and red that assembled together, make the view along the A19 better for everyone's health.

Project
MYSTERY CUBE
Architect
HAN SLAWIK

Project location   Hanover, Germany
Estimated use   Exhibition space
Container type   Building container

01

02

03

This temporary pavilion can be assembled, disassembled and reassembled to serve as exhibition space. Since no floor space could be allocated in the forum of Hanover's State Museum for educational projects related to The Mysterious Bog People exhibition, Slawik designed an external space housed in recycled building containers that were not immediately legible as such to the public. The containers were first stacked, surrounded by standard steel-tube scaffolding and then dressed in a black fiberglass textile. The result was a 7-meter cube rotated in such a way that it stood out clearly amongst the surrounding city fabric. Unlike most traveling show pavilions, Mystery Cube's standardized components facilitate its international transport by land or sea.

04

01-03
Mystery Cube deployed in a
Hanover plaza, supplementing
exibition space at the State
Museum.
04
The structure consisted of
three layers.

DERCUBE

LHVH
ARCHITEKTEN

Project location Freudenberg, Germany
Estimated use   Exhibition space
Container type   Building container

01

04

01
The temporary exhibition space
became sheer at night through
a textile cladding.
02, 03
During the day it looked
opaque and monolithic, since
fabric walls, which were later
recycled, hid the 36 containers making up the three-story
structure.
04
Entrance to the building.
05, 06
Floor plans.

02

03

derCube was a three-month extension to an exhibition that outgrew its event space in Freudenberg in the south of North Rhine-Westphalia. A three-story cube with approximately 400 square meters (4,305 square feet) of floor area was assembled on the market square in the town's historical center using 36 containers. The modular cube was distinguished by its unusual textile facade, which was made up of polyester strips coated with PVC. As it wrapped the underlying container grid, it disguised the modularity of its construction, creating the impression of a seamless and monolithic cube. When the exhibition was over, the containers were used again as office space, and the cloth facade was recycled. Through this project, the architects explored the ways in which a town can be shaped and altered by temporary structures. They discovered that the potential of certain locations can be revealed through temporary interventions; at the same time, new interpretations of existing structures also become imaginable.

05

06

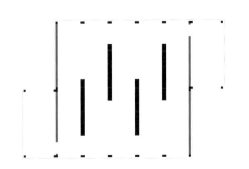

CARGO
GROUP 8

Project location   Vernier, Switzerland
Estimated use   Office
Container type   Freight container

01
Informal meeting space
between the containers.
02
Industrial texture contrasting
with the white interiors.
03
Workspace inside one of the
containers.
04
Drawing showing the composition of the containers
beside the desk area.
05
The office building itself is
a repurposed industrial space.
06
Staff holding breakout sessions
throughout the containers and
office space.

06

A former industrial space measuring 780 square meters (8,395 square foot) located outside Geneva was hollowed out and transformed into a large office space. Capitalizing on the structure's soaring nine-meter-high ceilings, 16 recycled shipping containers were inserted to punctuate the environment. The structure is inspired by Marcel Duchamp's concept of the "readymade", offering a new function for the containers. They are stacked up into a bi-level structure—"piled up as giant Lego", in the words of the architects. In the otherwise neutral grey and white office surroundings, the containers create a sense of texture and visual intrigue. The outer surfaces remain scuffed from their previous purpose, with their former logos and identification numbers still visible. But it is more than a visual decision: each container has assumed a specific use, such as meeting room, cafeteria, lounge, and bathrooms. The cluster of containers sits in contrast to the building's open space and glass roof, while the recesses between containers are used as pockets for informal meetings.

Project location Munich, Germany
Estimated use Showroom
Container type Building container

01
A textile made this grid of containers look uniform.
02
Some of the building containers used were stripped to their frames.
03
During the day, the pavilion looked opaque; as night fell, it revealed its layers.
04
Views in section.

01

02

03

This trade fair stand by LHVH featured 16 containers in the shape of a grid with additional boxes stacked to create an interior building of 27 containers ranged over three floors. The interiors included reception and café, stairs and a roof terrace. Another assemblage of 21 containers surrounded the inner booth with some stripped to their steel supporting skeletons, leaving a three-dimensional structure of x, y, z coordinates. After assembly, the components were sheathed in a vinyl mesh printed in a color that created a peaceful atmosphere. During the day, the stand's exterior was opaque—a quiet, impenetrable, minimalist box— as night fell, the shell became sheer to reveal its sculptured interior. Following the seven-day event, each container was returned to its original function.

04

50,000€ MODULAR-HOUSE
MM+P / MEYER-MIETHKE & PARTNER

Project location   Leipzig, Germany
Estimated use   Office and private residence
Container type   Container frames

01–03
This modular steel home was made from modified building containers with copious incisions that allowed designers to insert windows all around.
04
Looking down from the first floor.
05
The double-height interior and views that connect the home to its surroundings.

A 70-square-meter (753-square-foot), cube-based modular home made of steel and glass for less than €100,000? This kind of affordability was a product of mm+p architects clever choice to combine a high degree of prefabrication and standardization with a super-efficient layout. The designers worked with a limited range of material formats—incorporating only two glazing sizes, for example—and a simple flat roof made from steel sheeting that doubles as a water collection basin. The design places living,

cooking and eating areas on the first floor in such a way that they seem to form a single unit with the garden and terrace, even when the windows are closed. It is the glassy transparency that dissolves the boundaries of the house almost completely.

Project
OCEANSCOPE
Architect
ANLSTUDIO

Project location   Incheon City, South Korea
Estimated use   Observation deck
Container type   Freight container

01

02

Incheon City has one of South Korea's biggest ports, where more than three million containers move in and out of the harbor every year. Situated on a small plot adjacent to the sea, five containers fanning towards the sky and sea are fixed in place. An initiative by the mayor of Incheon City, Oceanscope explores the potential of containers repurposed as public spaces. This structure offers room for temporary exhibitions and an observation deck. AnL Studio first observed the ways in which containers were used throughout Korea, most often as temporary shelters in rural areas, and found these to be bleak and uninviting. Its response was to create a dynamic space that harmonized with the local surroundings. The structure utilizes its modest plot by positioning the containers on an angle, adding much-needed height to the observation deck. A series of slender windows appear like patterns from the outside, while filling the observation decks with light on the inside. The viewer can walk up the stairs in the slanting container to the observation deck and watch the sun set over the sea.

04

05

01
Oceanscope framing views of
the harbor and setting sun.
02
Stairs leading to the viewing
deck.
03
Three containers form viewing
points, while two more create
exhibition space.
04
The containers's angles allow
the viewer to observe the
setting sun from different
heights.
05
Inside the container
structure.

TEMPORARY ACCOMMODATION FOR 1001 DAYS

MEYER EN VAN SCHOOTEN ARCHITECTEN

Project location   Amsterdam, the Netherlands
Estimated use   Office space
Container type   Freight container

02

01

03

04

A large factory hall on the former site of the Stork engineering company was converted over a period of two months into an office by the architects who would inhabit it for the next few years. Blue freight containers were stacked in the vast 800-square-meter (8,611-square-foot) interior. The re-used freight containers not only formed rooms within the room but helped to define the space as a whole. The containers also had the virtue of gracefully expressing the temporary nature of the accommodation. Meyer en Van Schooten Architecten thrust a container through the outer wall to create the entrance. On the longitudinal axis of the shed, where it was tallest, they placed two structures, one

consisting of four containers and the other of two. The largest block, in which the ends of alternating containers were replaced by glass, contained the secretarial office and a conference room. The smaller block contained the network server and archives. Elsewhere, container clusters housed a model workshop, the lunch area, kitchen, sanitary facilities, a library, and management offices. The units were fitted with sliding walls and ceilings made of translucent plastic panels to create privacy and diminish distractions from without, while retaining heat during the winter.

01
The former factory building in which the architects inserted their temporary offices.
02, 03
Freight containers created rooms on the factory floor for everything from meeting space and a model workshop to offices and a library.
04
Some container walls were replaced with glass, sliding walls or ceilings made from translucent plastic.
05
An area for model display.
06
Ground floor plan.
07
Plan for the first floor.

06

07

Project

VOLVO C30 EXPERIENCE PAVILION

Architect

KNOCK

Project location   Gotheburg, Sweden
Estimated use   Showroom and event space
Container type   Freight container

Stockholm-based architects Knock designed this pavilion to present Volvo's 2006 C30 model to more than 6,000 dealers at the company's annual eight-week convention. Characterizing the car through oppositions—as more emotional than rational, raw yet smooth and having attitude while still being a Volvo—the architects emphasized contrasts, placing unpolished materials, beside clean, white surfaces, for instance. Each area of the event was assigned a distinct audio and visual code, built on these contrasts and built in the shape of the EKG line of a beating heart. Situated in an old boat shed in the rural harbor outside Gothenburg, the pavilion was accessed through a dim, 50-meter tunnel made from containers illuminated with LED strips only. In the main hall, dealers found the broader walls lined with rusty containers

stacked three high whose shorter ends served as projection screens. A 150-meter white conveyor belt wound through the room bearing hors d'oeuvres, along with objects identified as being of particular interest to the model's youthful target demographic. The participants were never allowed to see the car. Instead, every element of the pavilion interiors reflected the C30 in some way, giving the expectant audience all the clues needed to piece together an image of it in their minds.

01
Visitors entered through a 50-meter
tunnel of containers.
02
Raw corrugated metal was paired with
immaculate white. A conveyor belt
carried hors d'oeuvres.

CPH VILLAGE
ARCGENCY

Project location   Copenhagen, Denmark
Estimated use   Residential
Container type   Freight container

01

02

CPH Village is a company with a mission to combat the housing crisis, and to do so in a flexible, forward-thinking way. Local architecture practice Arcgency was enlisted to help bring that vision to life with a modular student village. The result is a series of temporary student residences. Temporary, because the only vacant and affordable land in Copenhagen is located in former industrial areas, with restrictive zoning that only allows for impermanent construction. Therefore, the structures needed to be easy to disassemble and move to a new location, a quality afforded to the architects by repurposed containers. Each 12-meter container comprises a shared entrance and bathroom, and two private rooms each with a sleeping area and kitchenette. With metal walls and almost three-meter-high ceilings, residents can personalize their spaces and hang items from the walls with magnets. At the center of the student village, a large flexible space—composed of three containers stacked atop one another—offers the students a communal space to cook, do laundry, and host social events.

01
Temporary student housing
on land eventually slated
for redevelopment.
02, 04
Shared and outdoor spaces
foster a sense of community.
03
Each container makes up
a cozy student residence.
05
CPH Village is created as
a low-density area with
buildings no higher than
two stories.

04

05

06, 07
Although the individual units
are small, the village is rich
with amenities throughout the
common spaces.
08
The industrial character is
complemented by the students
personalizing their units and
decorating the common spaces.
09
The spaces between the houses
are sheltered by a roof to
create outdoor living rooms.
10
The gates on either side of
the building open up to the
surrounding community.

Project
NOMADIC MUSEUM
Architect
SHIGERU BAN
ARCHITECTS

Project location   New York City, New York, USA
Estimated use   Exhibition space
Container type   Freight container

01

01
Exploded view of 148 containers that formed this floating
gallery.
02
The Nomadic Museum greeted
visitors on a New York City
pier, combining recycled and
ecofriendly materials for
which Ban is famous.

Tokyo-based architect Shigeru
Ban didn't reify the freight container
in his temporary nomadic museum;
instead, he used it pragmatically to
construct the cathedral-like exhibition
space. It took 148 multicolored shipping containers to raise the structure
at the edge of the Hudson River
at Pier 54 in Manhattan, and to
demonstrate the architect's command
of both materials and sustainable
practices. The 3,020-square-meter
(32,507-square-foot), four-story floating
and movable mammoth featured a
PVC membrane roof and walls, as well
as plywood walls, columns built from
water-sealed paper tube (a feature of
many of the architect's most famous
works), wood plank decking, and
300 tons of gravel that gave the project
an Eastern sensibility.

Famous for the use of paper in his architecture, Ban also suspended a sheer handmade curtain made of one million pressed paper Sri Lankan tea bags 40 feet above a wooden walkway that begins at the entrance, and in combination with the gravel, tightly controlled circulation through the show. Walls and partitions throughout the space were filled with Ashes and Snow, a multimedia exhibit by artist Gregory Colbert that included 199 large-scale photographs and a one-hour 35-millimeter film.

The surreal projected portraits of animals and humans felt at home in the post-industrial cathedral in which narrowly targeted lighting left the edges of the space dim and allowed the corrugated metal surfaces of the containers to recede into darkness.

03
The museum seen against the Manhattan skyline from the Hudson River.
04
The architect's signature paper tubes served as cathedral-scale columns, creating an arcade and naves that limited circulation.
05
Photographs were suspended, floating, between columns above 300 tons of gravel.
06
A view in section: Carefully focused lighting made the raw metal walls fade into darkness, leaving more refined elements in the foreground.
07
Site plan.

DRIVELINES STUDIOS

LOT-EK

Project location	Johannesburg, South Africa
Estimated use	Residential
Container type	Freight container

01

02

03

04

05
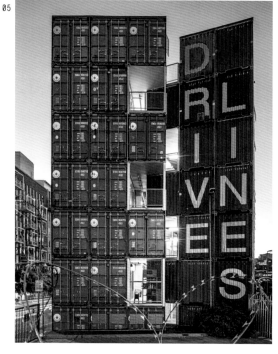

Drivelines Studios is situated in downtown Johannesburg, in an area recently revitalized by the post-apartheid generation—and this seven-floor residential building was a key catalyst in the neighborhood's regeneration. The modular structure is made up of 140 upcycled shipping containers, each selected in part for its color (the intention being that the containers wouldn't require a coat of paint). Instead, the identity is forged from the containers' original markings and color. The containers were stacked and cut on-site to form the residential units, each one an open-plan studio between 27–56 square meters (300–600 square feet) in size. The containers facing the street and courtyard have long diagonal windows that form a pattern along the facade. Drivelines Studios is built on a triangle-shaped plot. Two separate volumes are hinged together at the plot's narrow end, creating an open space in the middle for the residents to use as a communal outdoor area. The facades along the interior courtyard are articulated with staircases, an elevator tower, and a series of bridges that connect all levels. The ground level is used for residential units, as well as retail along Albertina Sisulu Road.

06

07

01
Drivelines Studios from
street level.
02
Drivelines Studios in
context with its wider
inner-city surroundings.
03
Containers are cut to form
windows and graphic patterns
along the facade.
04, 05, 06
A series of bridges and
staircases articulate the
interior facades.
07
Drivelines Studios by night.

08
Two residents overlooking
the interior courtyard.
09, 10
Interiors.
11
The two volumes frame a
social space at the center.

PAPERTAINER MUSEUM

SHIGERU BAN ARCHITECTS + KACI INTERNATIONAL INC.

Project location   Seoul, Korea
Estimated use   Exhibition space
Container type   Freight container

01

02

03

Ban's temporary exhibition pavilion built with cargo containers and paper tubes, was created in the Seoul Olympic Park on the occasion of the 30th anniversary of the Korean publisher Design House. Born in Tokyo in 1957, Ban studied architecture at the Southern California Institute of Architecture and the Cooper Union School of Architecture in New York and then worked for Arata Isozaki in Tokyo before founding his own practice in 1985. He began to explore the structural use of paper at different scales in 1985 and in greater earnest began to use paper tubes in the 1989 Paper Arbor in Nagoya. The site of the oddly named Papertainer Museum is encircled by a forest and a roundabout, anchored with a big sculpture at its center. All of the features of the site give it the shape of the letter "D" in plan, which, conveniently, also represents the first initial of the name of the client, which requested that Ban create two types of gallery in the 3,820-square-meter (41,118-square-foot) pavilion: one, a multipurpose space and gallery in which to hang large photography and, at the front part of the building, the Container Gallery. The Container Gallery is defined by two parallel walls, each approximately 10 meters high and made in a checker-board composition. Atop the steel-framed walls, like cross beams or a lid over the gallery below, Ban stacked ten 40-foot shipping containers. One container wall is used for exhibition booths and the second as office and storage spaces. The Semicircular Pavilion, also called the Paper Gallery, is composed of two circular walls made of Ban's signature paper tubes which serve as 75-centimeter posts, and support a roof truss that is also constructed from paper tubes.

04

01, 04
The museum facade with colonnades consisting of paper columns fronting a container gallery, office and storage space.
02, 05
The hemispherical plan of the building seen from overhead and in floor plan.
03
Inside, cardboard cylinders, gravel and a wooden walkway suggest the meditative atmosphere of a house of worship.
06 [pages 228–229]
Inside the textured and softly illuminated Container Gallery.

05

Project
CRUISE CENTER
Architect
RENNER HAINKE WIRTH ARCHITEKTEN

Project location	Hamburg, Germany
Estimated use	Cruise terminal
Container type	Freight container, container frames

01

01
The terminal's trapezoidal, illuminated roof makes a visual allusion to a white canvas sail.
02
The interior recalls a ship deck and the industrial vitality of the port.
03
A translucent foil applied to the container-lined facade makes the surfaces shine at night.

Hamburg-based architects Renner Hainke Wirth Architekten (RHWA) designed this temporary cruise terminal, taking their cues from two familiar elements of seafaring: the traditional overseas cargo container and the large, white canvas sail (which doubles nicely as a symbol for the luxurious, active life that includes shipboard holidaying). The corporate identity of the terminal came from a combination of the building's rough shell, assembled from existing container components, and a vast cantilevered roof that faces the city. A bright tarmac surface covered with colored carpet-like sections recalls a ship's deck and corresponds with the brightness of the shining white roof. At night, the roof resembles an illuminated and floating sheet of canvas while nearby, a grid of vertical

container follies also shine through the darkness due to the application of a translucent foil that inspired RHWA to dub them "lighthouses". The containers are painted in a range of maritime shades of blue. In contrast, their interior of the building is lined with a red floor. Like a window on the city, a wide opening in the terminal's facade directs the eyes of arriving cruise ship passengers to the city's skyline and towards Hamburg's renowned St. Michaelis Church.

04
The heavy cantilever of the
roof is as striking an image
as the gargantuan cruise ships
that resemble cities floating
impossibly on the sea.
05
The ship-shape bareness of
the interior and a view to the
water.
06
Section with roof structure.
07
Floor plan.

FLYPORT

WOLFGANG LATZEL ARCHITEKTEN

WOLFGANG LATZEL, NORBERT ZSCHORNACK

Project location   Various
Estimated use   Passenger terminal
Container type   Container frames

This standardized passenger terminal consisting of approximately 400 modules is laid out for 0.5 to 1.5 million passengers a year. The modular concept based on the standardized 20-foot container enables transport via truck, train, ship, and aircraft. Thanks to its modular design, the flyport not only ensures an extremely short realization time; its great adaptability in regard to the respective requirements also allows for flexible usage and individual design. Especially in times of dynamic increase in passenger capacities, the passenger terminal system offers a quick, flexible and individual solution. The flyport is delivered to sites in Europe, Asia, Africa, Latin America, the Caribbean, the Pacific region, and North America. Three standards have been developed: high, medium and basic standard, depending on the demands of the user or operator. High standard is for permanent regional airport operations, medium standard was developed for both permanent and temporary expansion terminals, while the basic design is aimed at the low-cost terminal market.

01
Exterior view of the passenger terminal with three levels.
02
Interior view of the main hall.
03
View of two-levelled passenger terminal.
04
Building sections.

COOL COOL SEASIDE

Architect

ATELIER LET'S

Project location   Kaohsiung City, Taiwan
Estimated use   Pavilion
Container type   Freight container

01

02

03

01
The pinewood flooring was especially selected to create a sense of relaxation.
02
The pavilion seeks toredefine the square as a living space.
03
The pre-existing reinforced concrete seats were absorbed into the foundation.
04
The aerial view shows how the container walls are used as sunshades.

A bustling high street made up of delis and dessert shops, and a pier leading to regional ferries. Wedged between the two is a small urban neighborhood that Taiwan's Urban Development Bureau wanted to revitalize; creating a public recreational space was part of the brief. In response, Atelier Let's created a striking pavilion from shipping containers and situated them at the center of a series of basketball courts painted in a riot of colors by a local graffiti artist. The containers extend over the courts like a canopy, to provide shady respite for spectators and passersby alike. The canopy's sight lines point towards a nearby temple. Due to constraints in both budget and time, the architects settled on cargo containers. The side panels were made into sunshades and the frames into structural supports, which were then lifted up by H-shaped columns erected adjacent to the concrete seats. The hard surfaces are offset by pinewood flooring to create a relaxing environment that welcomes the neighborhood's inhabitants to take a seat.

Project
HIDDEN VALLEY
Architect
MARMOL RADZINER PREFAB

Project location   Moab Desert, Utah, USA
Estimated use   Private residence
Container type   Container frames

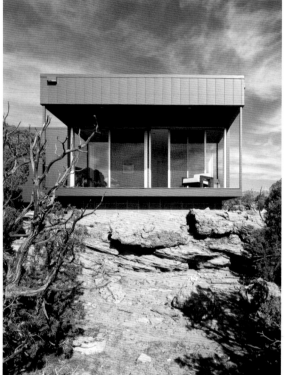

Los Angeles-based architects Marmol Radziner designed their Hidden Valley prefabricated house as a single-family vacation home near Moab, Utah. The firm's careful siting, emphasis on overlapping indoor and outdoor living, and integration of sustainable design elements celebrate and make the most of the area's inimitable access to nature. The 230-square-meter (2,475-square-foot) dwelling includes a 160-square-meter (1,722-square-foot) terrace and sits on an open, hundred-acre site punctuated by red rock formations and desert cliffs. Its two-bedroom, two-bath structure consists of five interior modules, seven ipe-wood deck modules and three additional modules making up the garage, all of which were fabricated in a factory and shipped fully assembled. In the factory, precut steel beams and joists were welded together to create the floor and roof frames. Pre-cut columns were attached to the floor frame and the roof structure was placed atop the columns. Then workers installed structurally insulated panels (SIPs) to form the sub-floor and roof structures. Once the steel frame was set, the interior wall framing, plumbing, and electrical and mechanical components were installed. Finally, they added windows and doors, interior and exterior finishes, built-in casework, appliances, and fixtures. The modules were then transported to the site on flatbed trucks, lifted onto the foundation with a crane, bolted together and welded to the foundation to create a permanent structure.

01–03
The prefab house peers over a desert cliff in Utah.
04
Site plan: Careful situating of the house allowed the team to integrate indoor and outdoor living.

05
The two-bedroom house consists of 15 factory-built modules.
06
A living room-cum-deck with pool.
07
Floor plan.

Project
CONTAINERWERKSTATT
Architect
GRIMME ARCHITEKTUR & MÖBELWERKSTÄTTEN

Project location   Münster, Germany
Estimated use   Office and manufacture
Container type   High cube freight container

01

From the outside, it might not look like much. Sixteen rust-red shipping containers stacked two high, but on the inside, German architecture practice and cabinet-maker Grimme has created a workspace that is clad in timber and filled with light. The space works as a furniture showroom, a workshop for joinery manufacture, a material library, and an office for a team of architects. The space, designed by and for Grimme, was created with a simple mission: to be the best place to work. Inside, the containers are concealed with pine plywood and articulated with glass. The containers themselves are not welded together; instead, they are connected through a mechanism behind the plywood.

The ground floor was also built in a way that it could be moved if needed. The location within Münster was strategically selected to eschew expen-sive city center rents, instead positioned in the harbor quarter just beside the canal, a site that corresponds well to the choice in materials.

01
The stacked containers
opening out to the
porch and terrace.
02
Warm timber interiors.
03
Manufacturing facilities
inside.
04, 05
The office interior.

04

05

Project
STACK II
Architect
ARCGENCY

Project location   Copenhagen, Denmark
Estimated use   Office
Container type   High cube freight container

01

01
Temporary workspace
overlooking the
Copenhagen harbor.
02
Side elevation.
03
Floorplan showing
office configurations.
04, 05
The interior uses
open spaces and
windows to create
a collaborative
environment with
quiet pockets.

02

03

High-quality, sustainable, and easy to assemble and disassemble, Stack II is a temporary office building erected on a piece of land that is slated for redevelopment. Once that moment comes, the building will be taken down and built elsewhere, or the materials will be reused for a new project. For the time being, the structure overlooks the Copenhagen harbor alongside Arcgency's previous container office building, Stack I, both offering accessible office space for start-ups and young businesses. Sustainability is at the heart of this scheme. The structure is built from 90 per cent recyclable materials, with natural ventilation, triple-layered windows and high-performance insulation panels clinging to the outside of the container, leaving its ridged walls visible on the inside. The checker-box formation of the six-meter high cube containers leaves a series of flexible voids that can be adapted on an ongoing basis. The structure itself is lifted off the ground on pillars, a decision that causes minimal impact on the site and makes the building easier to move.

06
The building is lifted off
the ground on pillars, with
insulated sandwich panels that
encapsulate the building on
all sides.
07
Section drawing. The tower on
the right marks the entrance
and serves as a fire escape.
08
The structure is built from
two rows of containers
stacked three stories high.
09
Stack II is expected to be in
its location overlooking the
harbor for 10–12 years.

08

Project
CONTAINER BAR
Architect
NORTH ARROW STUDIO

Project location   Austin, USA
Estimated use   Hospitality
Container type   Freight container

The generously sized Container Bar is a downtown Austin watering hole that is true to its name. The bar, a collaboration between North Arrow and Hendley Knowles design studio, was constructed by stacking seven shipping containers in an irregular formation—the materials were trucked into downtown Austin's Rainey Street district in several pieces. The result is a series of outdoor and enclosed seating areas that suit a variety of events and varying degrees of intimacy or exposure within a single venue. The containers are connected by concrete and concrete block, rusty plate steel, and chain link which preserves the wholly industrial look of Container Bar from the street. Inside, the industrial edge of the containers was completely transformed when floor, ceiling and walls were clad with timber planks and small tiles. The combination yields a warren of spaces that feel both rustic and modern. Each interior space has its own identity, decorated with comfortable furnishings in a vibrant color palette. At the center, a floating roof shelters a double-height bar from the elements while allowing the designers to populate this courtyard area with trees and greenery.

02

03

01
A double-height outdoor
bar shelters under a
floating roof.
02
The containers are stacked
strategically to optimize
a combination of indoor-
outdoor experiences.
03
The narrow interiors are
diverse and cozy with large
windows or glass doors.
04
The industrial boxes are
lined inside with rustic
timber and tiles.

04

Project
IBA_DOCK
Architect
HAN SLAWIK

PROJECT PARTNER: HENNER WINKELMÜLLER
WITH IMS INGENIEURSGESELLSCHAFT MBH AND BOF ARCHITEKTEN

Project location   Hamburg, Germany
Estimated use   Office and exhibition space
Container type   Container frames

01

02

04

01, 02
Section and floor plan
of the floating museum.
03
View from the dock.
A bridge leads to
the entrance on the
top floor.
04
View from the bridge.
05
Exhibition space.

Germany's largest floating building bobs up and down on a grid of so-called "dolphin piles" drifting approximately 3.5 meters daily on the tide and riding atop the water through extreme storms. The building is made up of a 45×25 meter concrete pontoon that serve as jetties and create a usable floor space of 1,600 square meters (17,222 square feet) over three stories. A bridge leads to the entrance on the top floor, accessing exhibition and presentation areas, a city model, cafeteria and an outdoor terrace. The modular steel frames can be disassembled for storage on land when the dock needs to pass under low bridges while being towed for maintenance work. These frames were prefabricated, transported by road, and then assembled in two weeks over the pontoon. The container modules can be easily converted at any time without having to change load bearing parts. Equipped to draw on the sun and the Elbe river for energy, the resulting building does not require any additional external power source.

Project
SANLITUN SOUTH
Architect
LOT-EK

Project location   Beijing, China
Estimated use   Retail and office space
Container type   Freight container

01

02

05

03

Beijing's four-story, 24,000-square-meter (258,834-square-foot) Sanlitun South mall is strung with shipping containers, orange-painted, stainless-steel mesh, and steel scaffolding—a form reminiscent of the medieval Chinese hutong—a quarter tightly packed with low-slung buildings threaded with alleys, elevated pathways and courtyards. New York-based LOT-EK designed the northeast section of this retail "village" to be filled with retail, restaurants and event spaces by threading it with multilevel, open-air circulation routes and 151 containers. In the alleys, the designers wedged a network of metal frames between the buildings, connecting them along the side of the buildings by a system

of horizontal metal rods that serve as both railings and a brise-soleil, and creating a loggia on the upper levels. The texture of the structure derives from the standard eight-foot width of the ISO shipping containers that were plugged into the facade of the building in such a way that they stick out into the alleys and serve as canopies at the ground level: awnings on the exterior and places to display objects in shop interiors. On the higher floors, the containers are sliced through with circulation routes, forming entrances to stores or display windows and functioning everywhere as graphic objects tattooed with signage.

01, 02
The plan was based on that of the midieval Chinese hutong, a dense quarter threaded with alleys and bridges.
03, 07
Elevations.
04-06
Cargo containers jut out of the seemingly ordinary building forming shading outside and retail awnings within.

07

Project
CONTAINER STACK PAVILION
Architect
PEOPLE'S ARCHITECTURE OFFICE

Project location   Taiyuan, China
Estimated use   Pavilion
Container type   Freight container

01

01
Stacked containers form
a zigzag pattern.
02
The containers are stacked
to form roof terraces
and shaded outdoor spaces.
03
The short side of the containers
are floor-to-ceiling windows
to allow sight lines throughout
the building.
04, 05
People engaging with the
public space.

02

03

Container Stack Pavilion is a temporary structure that can be disassembled and moved from location to location. Its inaugural position is in the northern Chinese city of Taiyuan, near Beijing. The perpendicular containers, painted in a cheerful palette of red and yellow to command attention and stand out from their surroundings, are stacked atop one another in an angular procession to maximize rooftop views, as well

as the area beneath where the public can seek shade. Where the two levels overlap, a double-height atrium is carved out of the containers to create an airy and welcoming public space. Visitors enter through what the architects describe as a "7.5-meter cantilevered box" to access the building's upper level, while the pavilion itself extends outwards to the bordering streets, where passersby can catch a glimpse of the activity inside.

Full-height glazing at the end of each container allows natural light to flow through the space, as well as create lines of sight throughout the pavilion. The zigzagging floorplan creates corners for pockets of seating where visitors can rest their legs and enjoy the vibrant, primary-colored space.

06
Aerial view showing the
composition of the stacked
containers.
07, 08
Overlapping containers form
a double-height atrium.
09
The upper decks extend
outwards to over the nearby
street, showcasing the
activities going on inside.
10
Second-floor seating.

Project

RESEARCH STATION

Architect

IMS INGENIEURGESELLSCHAFT MBH AND BOF ARCHITEKTEN

Project location   Larsemann Hills, Antarctica
Estimated use   Research station
Container type   Building container

container

+

skin

=

research base

01

02

01
The formula for combining the station's layers: a grid of footed containers wrapped in a sleek, aerodynamic skin.
02
Longitudinal and cross section.

03
Using containers was a response to challenges of the site's extreme climate, terrain and remoteness.
04
Floor plan.

Bof Architekten were responding to extreme climate conditions and limited transport opportunities in designing this research station on a peninsula in the Larsemann Hills region of the northeastern Antarctic. Furthermore, because of the site's poor accessibility and the restrictions set forth by the Antarctic Treaty, it was crucial that the station be completely self-sufficient. The prefabricated building, which was shipped in discrete components and then assembled on site, came with its own energy supply and water preparation and treatment facilities. Assembly could only be carried out during the extremely brief Antarctic summer, but once completed, houses 25 researchers and scientists during the warm months and 15 in winter. The building consists of 132 containers, the superb mobility and flexibility of which make it well-suited to transport and short assembly times. The boxes' various programs are clearly structured and separated: The first floor features living areas with 24 single and double rooms, a kitchen and dining area, a small library, storage and washing rooms, a fitness space, offices and a lounge. Underneath, on the ground floor, the containers house laboratories, storage, equipment rooms (including the central energy unit), and a garage with a workshop. The deliberate compactness of the interiors makes for short access distances, resulting in short piping and wiring lengths. Due to low temperatures and strong winds, the containers are jacketed with an aerodynamic shell of metal panels, optimized for the prevailing climate. In terms of energy, waste heat from the CHP units is harnessed and used to heat the station, but the building also has three combined heat and power units for back-up electrical purposes. In addition, it is fitted with ventilation and air-conditioning equipment that maintain a humidity level of 30%. Windows at each end give views from the dining area and lounge onto vast expanses of ice and sea. Inside, the generous use of wood, color and ample lighting cultivate a warmer and less isolating live-work atmosphere.

04

RAUSCH SCHOKOLADEN COCOA ESTATE

Architect

CONTAINERWERK

Project location   Tres Equis, Costa Rica
Estimated use   Research and residential
Container type   Freight container

01

02

03

04

01
The Rausch chocolate company's research station in the Costa Rican jungle.
02
The containers are stacked to create a roof terrace.
03
Dining space inside.
04
One of the containers on the ground floor makes up the lavatory and shower.
05
Solar panels on the roof are part of a wider sustainability strategy to disturb the jungle as little as possible.
06
The building's exterior.

06

Four of Rausch Schokoladen's shipping containers were transported by sea from the port of Hamburg to Puerto Limón in Costa Rica. Once a means to transport cocoa beans across the world's oceans, they now form living and research units for the German chocolate company deep in the Costa Rican jungle. The structure was built in a way to create minimal impact on the surrounding environment. The prefabricated structure contains four shipping containers, which were aesthetically, structurally, and technically fitted out before being transported to the site. This means that, once on site, it only took four days to assemble the building ensuring the sensitive jungle surroundings would face minimal noise pollution and construction debris. The base is constructed from two containers, which house the laboratory and bathing areas for the workers. Another two, stacked on top, are where the sleeping and living quarters are situated. The building is intended to be fully self-sufficient and solar powered. In a second building phase, a water treatment plant will be installed, ensuring the building can operate independently of the rain forest. Once it is no longer in use, it can easily be dismantled and removed from site.

Project

REDONDO BEACH HOUSE

Architect

DEMARIA DESIGN ASSOCIATES INC.

PETER DEMARIA WITH CHRISTIAN KIENAPFEL

Project location	Redondo Beach, California, USA
Estimated use	Private residence
Container type	Freight container

01

02

NORTH

01
Ground floor plan.
02
First floor plan.
03
DeMaria used freight containers, airplane hangar doors
and prefab roof panels to
supplement the otherwise conventional construction of this
Los Angeles area home.

Peter DeMaria built the Redondo Beach House from ISO cargo containers, amongst other materials, thus combining industrial materials usually not used for residential construction with materials employed by conventional building methods. The result is what he calls a "hybrid". Old containers, hangar doors, prefabricated roof panels, greenhouse multi-skinned acrylic sheets, formaldehyde-free plywood, sprayed insulating material, and tankless water heaters were used. Using containers appealed to the architect because of their robustness and because they are virtually mold and termite-proof. In his design, DeMaria drew on tried and tested mass products: from Frank Lloyd Wright's Textile Block homes and Andy Warhol's prints, all the way to McDonald's mass-production of hamburgers. His aim was bring more people closer to their dream of owning a high-quality custom home at an affordable price. "This project is the torchbearer for a new, more affordable method of design and construction," says DeMaria, "Architecture as a Product."

04
The backyard with
swimming pool and
large window surfaces.
05
The windows swing
upward to combine
living room with lawn.
06
Interior details.
07
The entrance
to the house.

Project
CHALET DU CHEMIN BROCHU

Architect
PIERRE MORENCY ARCHITECTE

Project location Beaulac-Garthby, Québec, Canada
Estimated use   Private residence
Container type   Freight container

01

02

03

04

The chalet's prefabrication began in Montreal with the acquisition of three used black containers, which were then transported to the site and suspended like immense beams amongst the trees. A second, more traditional wooden skin, made from local hemlock that was dried and hammer-marked with the help of a portable sawmill, was applied to join the metal boxes together.

06

07

08

09

01, 02
Three black cargo containers form the core of this second home but they are clad in a second skin made from strips of local hemlock wood.
03
Ground floor plan.
04
First floor plan.
05, 08
The rear deck is where the containers are most visible. Morency let them jut out slightly, emphasising their elegant placement, which makes the most of forest views.
06, 07
Interiors.
09
Longitudinal section.

The Hidden Valley residence features sustainable materials and systems to minimize the environmental impact of both its production and its use: geothermal systems use the earth to heat and cool the home, while solar panels draw energy from the sun. The home's recycled steel frame promises long-term durability against the elements, termites and even mold without requiring chemical treatments.

08
Kitchen and living room. The house draws on geothermal energy and solar panels.
09
A bedroom with views of red rock and blue sky. The reverence for nature isn't just expressed through views but through sustainable systems that power the dwelling.
10
In many ways, the sturdy recycled steel architectural frame becomes a picture frame in the dramatic landscape.

Project
HOUSE 28
Architect
STUDIO EDWARDS

Project location   Wye River, Australia
Estimated use   Residential
Container type   Freight container

01

04

02

03

01, 04
The containers are insulated
and clad with galvanized steel
sheeting.
02, 03
The warm and bright interiors
are lined with marine plywood.

For hikers passing by, House 28 might seem like a nondescript steel box on stilts in the middle of the forest—but that was exactly the intent. A weekend retreat, it is made from three six-meter shipping containers: two form a living space, toilet, laundry, and entrance hall; a further container makes up two bedrooms and a shower. The structure is elevated above the forest floor on steel stilts that sit on deep concrete pile foundations, which anchor the house to its sloping site. The exterior walls are insulated and covered with galvanized steel sheeting, and the interior walls are clad with blond marine plywood. To further insulate the home and help it blend with the landscape, the building is topped with a green roof of native plants. Connecting the trio of containers is an external south-facing deck, accessed via a series of double-glazed doors and windows. Here, inhabitants can enjoy views of the forest and the ocean in the distance between the trees.

ESCAPE DEN
RIVER & RAIN

Project location Dhaka, Bangladesh
Estimated use Residential
Container type Freight container

01

The Escape Den was designed by River & Rain with a challenge: to transform the austere, utilitarian sensibility of shipping containers into a cozy escape from the city. The home is situated on the outskirts of Bangladesh's bustling capital city on a green plot that was kept intentionally simple to celebrate the unexpected form of the building. To the architects, the structure standing in a central open space serves as an abstraction of the traditional rural Bengal courtyard. A steel skeleton frames overlapping shipping containers, which are softened by architectural details such as floating platforms and intertwining stairs. Locally manufactured materials are used throughout, starting with the structural element of the building's facade. The containers themselves were handpicked from the depot and the interiors are clad in engineered wood along floors and walls, painted in muted tones, and filled with minimal yet eclectic furniture. A screen was erected along one side of the deck for vegetation to create a living wall. Vines cover the roof and provide a buffer from the heat, while in the center of the space, an almond tree grows along the full-height of the three-story external atrium.

02

SECTION BB

03

01
The containers are
placed perpendicular
within a steel
frame skeleton.
02, 04
Technical sketches
from the architects.
03
Rust-proof repellent
was applied to preserve
the character of the
containers. The stairs
are made from reclaimed
shipping decks.

04

SECTION AA

05, 06, 07
The interior was designed
as a cozy counterpoint
to the industrial surfaces.
08
Escape Den is located on
the outskirts of Dhaka and
is envisaged as a peaceful
retreat from the city.

Project
TONY'S FARM
Architect
PLAYZE

Project location   Shanghai, China
Estimated use   Office and manufacture
Container type   Freight container

01

02

This fruit and vegetable farm strives to do more than provide the region with certified organic produce. It aims to invite the community to the complex itself, and to encourage a sustainable lifestyle. In addition to public spaces, the building also needed to provide offices, a VIP room, and facilities where produce can be prepared for distribution. Visitors enter the space through a three-story entrance hall that is linked to an inner courtyard, where a series of electric cars can whisk them around the farm. The spatial sequencing was designed to connect the building's disparate uses into a single open space, linked by a series of internal bridges and passageways. The design encourages transparency, so visitors gain a better understanding of where their food comes from. In keeping with the ethos of the organic farm, the structure followed a stringent sustainability program that included geothermal heating, insulation, external shading blinds, and LED lighting. The freight containers themselves were selected for being what the architects refer to as, "A common metaphor for 'recycled space'."

03

04   05

06

07

01, 02
The green containers of
the organic farm complex.
03
Exterior leading to
double-height entrance.
04
Section drawing of the tea
lounge, entrance, lobby,
and courtyard.
05
Section drawing showing the
terrace, office, exhibitions
space, and warehouse.
06
Double height entrance
and cafe area.
07
The complex also includes
an area dedicated to food
packaging.

Project
VINOFAKTUR VOGAU
Architect
BWM ARCHITEKTEN

Project location   Vogau, Austria
Estimated use   Hospitality and commercial
Container type   Freight container

01, 02, 03
The container-rooms of this
wine distribution center
and shop plug into an architectural framework like wine
bottles into a rack.
04
The concept made an aesthetic
virtue of the building's
storage function with each
container representing a
single product category.

A growing wine distribution business needed to expand. Two brothers based in Styria, a wine region in southeast Austria, decided the next step would be a wine shop and exhibition space where they could showcase regional culinary products. Vienna-based architects BWM went with the viticultural theme and built 60-meter long and 12-meter high steel framework that recalls an outsize wine rack and "stores" 14 shipping containers. This is intentional, the concept was to showcase, instead of concealing, the site's simultaneous function as a storage facility. It also makes a statement that ties the authenticity of the owner's products with the character of the architecture in which they're contained.

Ultimately, the building creates a striking visual landmark. The containers, are labeled with references to local products delivered from all over Styria and each represents a single product category, like wine, schnapps, oil or meat. At the highest point, the designers even installed a wine tavern. The intention for the structure is that the containers can be rearranged and reconfigured—to offer visitors new experiences, and to evolve alongside the needs of the Vinofaktur.

Project
SHELTAINERS
Architect
MOUAZ ABOUZAID,
BASSEL OMARA,
AND AHMED HAMMAD

Project location   Cairo, Egypt
Estimated use   Residential
Container type   Freight container

01

02

01
Renderings show how
container structures could
form a new neighborhood.
02, 03
Ample greenery would create
a new green lung for Cairo.
04, 05, 06
The Sheltainer concept clusters eight homes around
a central courtyard, with
a tower at the center.

Like many major cities, Egypt's capital is facing a housing crisis. As a result, makeshift shelters have started appearing in mass quantities in Cairo Necropolis, where residents dwell side-by-side with the dead. More than 1.5 million people are now living here, in the city's oldest burial site that dates back to the seventh century AD. Three UAE-based architects have explored the phenomenon and conceptualized a potential solution, one that re-houses the mostly low-income families, students, and refugees into sturdy homes made from shipping containers. The award-winning proposal envisions Sheltainers, a cluster of homes built around a central courtyard. The ultimate aim is for these neighborhoods to be zero waste, with wind turbines, water tanks, and solar panels all located in a tower at the center of the courtyard. The micro-housing concept capitalizes on the availability of shipping containers from nearby ports. Being home to the Suez Canal, Egypt has an abundance of ports on both the Mediterranean and Red Seas, the nearest being about an hour from the site.

08

OUTLOOK

With its numerous and varied architectural examples, this container atlas demonstrates quite clearly that containers are complex building modules that offer suitable solutions for a wide range of uses. The wide spectrum of architectural solutions involving containers, some of which are quite experimental, demonstrate a high und impressively consistent level of quality. The way in which containers are used as building modules appears to be opening up the possibility of a creative, sophisticated, almost playful manner of working with modular space. Unexpected solutions are being realized in unconventional ways and are attracting a lot of attention. The negative image of container buildings, which arose over the last decades due to temporary, low-quality structures, has long since been reversed. Construction based on containers is now "in". Spatial solutions that exploit the potential of these globalized vessels can now boast a progressive and intelligent image.

However, the development of these intelligent spatial solutions with (freight) containers or other related building systems definitely requires architectural input and expertise. For this to happen, background knowledge about the potential possibilities and also the limitations of container architecture is necessary; the potential and the limitations are also influenced by engineering constraints. The present compendium provides this knowledge that, because of the pace of developments in container architecture, actually needs to be continually updated. Every month, new and interesting container projects are being implemented; nonetheless, the fundamentals of working with containers remain universally valid.

How will the freight container sector develop in the future? Will there be developments that influence the use of containers in architecture? There is no doubt that international freight transportation is no longer conceivable without containerization. The integrated logistical tools used in shipping will not change again in a revolutionary way in the foreseeable future. The continued availability of freight containers as a building block is thus assured. Nonetheless, there are indications that the dimensions of containers, and thus also of transportation equipment, may need to be improved. Some changes have already been carried out in the past— for example, the introduction of the high cube format that was one foot (approx. 30 centimeters) higher, the isolated introduction of 45-foot-long containers, and the even less common widening of containers by a few centimeters to achieve the maximum of 2.5 meters allowed by German road traffic regulations. There are also other conceivable ways of further optimizing container transportation—e.g. the widespread use of flexible container types with folding, sliding, or flap mechanisms could help to save valuable space on return journeys. From 2020 on the storage of fright containers in terminals will additionally take place in racking systems— high bay warehouses. In this case, individual containers can be directly accessed. All these developments have influenced and continue to influence the use of containers in construction.

Container architecture has great potential with regard to sustainability. When viewed from an ecological perspective, container building blocks offer a lot of features that fulfill contemporary ideas regarding the absolute flexibility of spatial solutions: they are a variable and mobile minimal building block for extensions to existing buildings and for new projects, providing quick, inexpensive spatial solutions that can be converted, reused or recycled in a sustainable manner later on. "Container Architecture" thus has major potential for delivering adaptable building solutions that will remain relevant even when requirements change in the future.

09

APPENDIX

TIMELINE

INDEX OF IMAGES

BIBLIOGRAPHY

CONTAINERS IN GENERAL

Container Contacts – 2009 Edition (mit CD-ROM). 37. Auflage, Storck Verlag, Hamburg, 2009.

Kotnik, Jure: *Container Architecture: This Book Contains 6,441 Container.* Links books, Barcelona, 2008.

Kramer, Sybille: *STACK, CUT, ASSEMBLE ISO 668.* Braun Publishing, Salenstein, 2019

Smith, Courtenay / Topham, Sean: *Xtreme houses.* Prestel, München, 2002.

Siegal, Jennifer: *MOBILE: The Art of Portable Architecture.* Princeton Architectural Press, 2002.

Siegal, Jennifer: *More mobile: Portable Architecture for Today.* Princeton Architectural Press, 2008.

Topham, Sean: *Move House.* Prestel, München, 2004.

FREIGHT CONTAINERS

Beplat, Klaus: *Probleme der Einführung des Containerverkehrs.* Verlag Weltarchiv, Hamburg 1970.

Cudahy, Brian J.: *Box Boats: How Container Ships Changed the World.* Fordham Univ. Press, New York, 2006.

Eilers, Reimer: *Das neue Tor zur Welt: Vierzig Jahre Container im Hamburger Hafen.* mareverlag GmbH, Hamburg, 2009.

Gräfing, Birte / Heinrichs, Dirk (Hrsg): *Vom Stauhaken zum Container: Hafenarbeit im Wandel.* Kellner, Bremen, 2008.

International Organization for Standardization (Hrsg.): *Freight containers: ISO Standards Handbook.* ISO Central Secretariat, Genf, 2000.

Kalkin, Adam: *Architecture and Hygiene.* Batsford, London, 2002.

Kalkin, Adam: *Quik Build: Adam Kalkin's ABC of Container Architecture.* Bibliotheque McLean, London 2008.

Kienzle, Jörg: *Das Container-Transportsystem.* In: Schriftenreihe Transport und Verkehr 1, München, 1991.

Lamster, Mark / Tolla, Ada: *Urban Scan / LOT-EK.* Princeton Architectural Press, New York, 2002.

Levinson, Marc: *The Box: How the Shipping Container Made the World Smaller and the World Economy Bigger.* Princeton University Press, Princeton NJ, 2006.

Lindner, Erik: *Die Herren der Container: Deutschlands Reeder-Elite.* Hoffmann und Campe, Hamburg, 2008.

Pawlik, Thomas / Hecht, Heinrich: *Containerseeschifffahrt.* Heel Verlag GmbH, Königswinter, 2007.

Preuß, Olaf: *Eine Kiste erobert die Welt: Der Siegeszug einer einfachen Erfindung.* Murmann Verlag, Hamburg, 2007.

Scoates, Christopher / Neidhardt, Jane: *LOT-EK: Mobile Dwelling Unit.* D.A.P. Distributed Art Publishers, New York, 2003.

Sawyers, Paul: *Intermodal Shipping Container Small Steel Buildings.* 2005, 2008.

Smith, John: *Shipping Containers as Building Components, Resarch.* NA Brighton University, UK, School of the Built Environment, 2006.

Witthöft, Hans Jürgen: *Container: Eine Kiste macht Revolution.* Koehler, Hamburg, 2000.

Witthöft, Hans J.: *Container: Die Mega-Carrier kommen.* Koehler, Hamburg, 2004.

BUILDING CONTAINERS

Doßmann, Axel / Wenzel, Jan / Wenzel, Kai: *Architektur auf Zeit: Baracken, Pavillions, Container.* b_books Verlag, Berlin, 2006.

Uhde, Robert: *De Vijf: Student Housing in Utrecht, Netherlands – Living in a box.* In: Architektur aktuell, 5/2005, S. 86-91, Springer Verlag, Vienna.

CONTAINER FRAMES / MODULAR CONSTRUCTION

Bauwelt: *Modulbauhersteller in Deutschland,* 21.2018, Bauverlag BV GmbH, Berlin, 2018.

Deutsche BauZeitschrift DBZ 6/2018, Sonderheft Modulbau, Bauverlag BV GmbH, Gütersloh, 2018.

Dörries, Cornelia / Zahradnik, Sarah: *Container- und Modulbauten,* DOM publishers, Berlin, 2016.

Slawik, Han: *Modulbau–der Weg in die modulare Zukunft.* In: industrieBAU 2/2017, S. 34-36, FORUM Zeitschriften und Spezialmedien GmbH, Merching, 2017.

Staib, Gerald / Dörrhöfer, Andreas / Rosenthal, Markus: *Elemente und Systeme: modulares Bauen.* Birkhäuser, Edition DETAIL, Basel, 2008.

LIST OF COMPANIES

FREIGHT CONTAINERS

MANUFACTURERS

www.bslcontainers.com
BSL Container Manufacturer, Hongkong

www.containerparts.nl
Van Doorn Container Parts B.V., Rotterdam/
the Netherlands

www.dcmhl.com
DCM Hyundai Limited, Faridabad/India

www.hempel.com
Hempel A/S, Lyngby/Denmark;

www.sec-bremen.de
Ship's Equipment Centre, Bremen/Germany

www.singamas.com
Singamas Container Holdings Ltd., Shanghai/China

www.sino-peak.com
Sino-Peak Container Manufacturing Co. Ltd.,
Tianjin/China

DEALERS

www.alcu.de
Container und mobile Räume GmbH,
Seevetal/Germany

www.conical.de
CONICAL GmbH, Hamburg/Germany

www.finsterwalder-container.de
Finsterwalder Container GmbH,
Kaufbeuren/Germany

www.rainbow-containers.de
Rainbow Containers GmbH, Biedersdorf/Germany

www.renz-container.com
RENZ Handel & Logistik GmbH, Stuttgart/Germany

www.container.de
ELA Container GmbH, Haren (Ems)/Germany

BUILDING CONTAINERS

www.algeco.de
www.alho.com
www.bboxx.de
www.container.de
www.containerland.de
www.deutsche-industriebau.de
www.drehtainer.de
www.eberhardt.eu
www.kleusberg.de
www.modulplan.de
www.optirent-mietservice.de
www.raumsysteme.de
www.saebu.de
www.sbs-containerservice.de
www.flexotel.nl
www.portacabin.co.uk
www.containex.com
www.chv.at
www.ofc.cz
www.uniteam.se
www.swmobilestorage.com
www.triumphmodular.com
www.willscot.com (Trailer)
www.pacvan.com (Trailer)
www.goldenofficetrailers.com
www.jobsitemobileoffices.com

CONTAINER FRAMES/MODULAR CONSTRUCTIONS

www.kleusberg.de
www.ofra.de
www.alho.de
www.modbau.de
www.algeco.de
www.cadolto.com
www.eberhardt.eu
www.yorkon.co.uk
www.sekisuiheim.com
www.bolle.net
www.adk-modulraum.de
www.saebu-modulbau.de
www.adapteo.de

WOODEN CONSTRUCTION

www.induo.de
www.stugeba.at
www.modulbau-lingen.de
www.swisskrono.com
www.renggli-international.com
www.purelivin.net

HYBRID CONSTRUCTION

www.renggli-international.com
www.ursem.nl

ORGANIZATIONS

www.ansi.org
ANSI – American National Standards Institute

www.bic-code.org
ICB – International Container Bureau

www.containerhandbuch.de
Cargo Loss Prevention Information from German
Marine Insurers

www.din.de
DIN – Deutsches Institut für Normung

www.iata.org
IATA – International Air Transport Association

www.imo.org
IMO – International Maritime Organization

www.imo.org
CSC – The International Convention for Safe
Containers

www.marisec.org
ICS – International Chamber of Shipping

www.tis-gdv.de
TIS Transport Informations-Service –
Fachinformationen der deutschen
Transportversicherer

www.uic.asso.fr
UIC – International Union of Railway

www.unece.org
UN/ECE – United Nations Economic Commission
for Europe

REGULATORY WORKS

STANDARDS

ISO 668
Series 1 freight containers, classification
external dimensions and ratings
[Amd. 1993 (E)]

ISO 830
Terminology in relation to freight containers,
(Amd. 1988)

ISO 1161
Series 1 freight containers – corner fittings
Specification (Amd. 1990)

ISO 1496-1
Series 1 freight containers – specification
and testing Part 1: general cargo containers
for general purposes (Amd.2 – 1998)

ISO 3874
Series 1 freight containers – handling
and securing

ISO 6346
Freight containers coding, identification
and marking – 1995 (E)

ISO 8323
freight containers – Air/surface (intermodal)
general purpose containers – specification
and tests

ISO 8501-1
Preparation of steel substrates before application of paints and related products

ISO 12944
Paints and varnishes – corrosion protection of
steel structures by protective paint systems

GUIDELINES

Bundesgütegemeinschaft Montagebau und
Fertighäuser e.V. (Federal quality association
for prefabricated buildings), Germany

RAL quality mark
steel construction system

DIN 18800-7 and 18808
Major welding certificates

Regelmäßige Kontrollen und Optimierung der
Fertigung, Qualitätsstandard nach DIN EN ISO
9001 (Regular checking and optimization of
production, quality standard as per DIN EN ISO
9001) (TÜV certificate, DEKRA Certification
GmbH, Germany)

Surveys on the fulfillment of standards regarding statics, fire protection, noise protection

RGST 1992: Guidelines relating to the process of
applying for and receiving permission for the
transportation of bulky and heavy loads

EnEV 2020, Energy Savings Ordinance for
Buildings, Germany

GLOSSARY

20-FOOT CONTAINER
The most commonly used container size worldwide in the ISO dimensions l/w/h 20'/8'/8'6".

40-FOOT CONTAINER
Basic module for the standardization of ISO containers. Today, it is the most commonly used container size after the 20-foot container.

BRIDGE FITTING
Component for joining containers horizontally.

BSE
Building services equipment; i.e. heating system, electrical installation, sanitation, etc.

BUILDING SITE CONTAINER
Standardized building module with container dimensions based on the model of the freight container, but developed solely for building purposes.

CHASSIS
Undercarriage for supporting transport loads; a term mostly used in vehicle manufacture.

CLIMATE SHELL
Dividing envelope that also acts as an insulator by slowing heat exchange due to its heat transmission resistance.

CONTAINER BLOCK BEARINGS
Intermediate storage (stack) of containers in terminals, with bad access to single containers.

CONTAINER DIMENSIONS
Typical dimensions of containers according to the ISO standard, refers particularly to length dimensions quoted in units of feet (10 feet, 20 feet, 40 feet, etc.).

CONTAINER FRAME
Further development of existing container types with a consistent separation between frame and filling.

CONTAINER HIGH BAY STORAGE
Intermediate storage (shelving system), in which individual containers can be accessed directly.

CONTAINER LOOK
Architecture with replicated containers, i.e. conventionally constructed building components, the shape of which is reminiscent of containers.

COR-TEN STEEL
Very strong and weather-resistant steel alloy (CORrosion resistance and TENsile strength).

CORNER FITTING
Attachment points at all corners of a container. They serve as fastening points when lifting, stacking and securing a container.

CROSS MEMBER
Carrier beams made of steel profiles in the base of a container, which support transport loads.

DYNAMIC LOADS
Loads caused by movements (impact forces caused by sliding or loading of containers, for example).

ENEV
German Energy Saving Ordinance; regulations valid in Germany for the reduction of CO_2 emissions from buildings; the ordinance prescribes insulation and heating standards for new buildings.

FILLING
Flat, space-delimiting elements fitted to the supporting structure.

FLEXIBILITY
Ability to adapt to change.

FOOT
Imperial measurement unit originally related to the dimensions of the human foot. The metric conversion factor for the standard English foot is 1 foot = 0.3048 meters. Other derived measurement units are:
1 yard = 3 feet
1 foot = 12 inches
1 inch = 25.4 millimeters

FRAME
Supporting structure of a container, three-dimensional.

FREIGHT CONTAINER
General terms for reusable containers for transporting all types of goods.

GALVANIZATION
Process for providing corrosion protection for steel; the hot-dip galvanization process gives steel a surface coating of zinc; damaged areas must be treated again (cold galvanization).

GLUED-LAMINATED TIMBER
Extremely stable wood building material made of glued boards.

GOOSENECK CHASSIS
Low-based container chassis with a swan-neck coupling component that lowers the loading area height and improves road handling.

GRID
Linear layout pattern for buildings based on the repetition of common distances; there are numerous grid types, which can be identified based on geometry (line grids, band grids, etc.) or classification (structural grids, fittings grids, etc.); the definition of grids/building axes makes unique spatial classification possible.

HIGH CUBE
ISO container with a height of 9 feet and 6 inches; further standardized container heights are the standard cube (8 feet 6 inches) and the square-shaped low cube (8 feet).

HOT GALVANIZING
Corrosion protection by means of thermally applying a zinc coating on steel.

INDIVIDUALIZATION
Adaptation to specific requirements, specialization.

INSULATION
Material with a high heat transmission resistance that is used to reduce heat losses from a building.

ISO
Abbreviation for the International Organization for Standardization, which prepares internationally valid technical "Normung"standards.

ISO CONTAINER
Freight container that fulfils the specifications of the "ISO" ISO 668 standard.

LASHING
Securing systems for fastening containers during transport.

LOW CUBE
ISO container with a reduced height compared to the standard cube (8 feet).

MOBILITY
Movability, not tied to a fixed location.

MODULE
Individual unit in an overall system.

MODULE BUILDING (FRAME)
Container-like building system made of prefabricated room cells, closed or open, made of frames used as building modules; however, dimensions are different from container-ISO-dimensions. This design has established itself under the name "modular construction".

NOMINAL DIMENSION
Dimension for orientation that does not correspond with the actual size.

PIN FOUNDATION
Releasable point foundations made from prefabricated concrete parts.

PLYWOOD
Wooden panels consisting of a number of veneer layers bonded to each other in alternating directions at right angles.

PONTOON
Floating concrete or steel body on water that supports a building.

PREFABRICATION
Manufacturing process for building components that takes place in the workshop rather than on site; the greater the degree of prefabrication, the less work remains to be done on site.

PRIMARY SUPPORT STRUCTURE
Main components of the supporting structure that are largely responsible for carrying loads.

MAKESHIFT SOLUTION
Temporarily installed.

OPEN SYSTEM
Building system that is combinable with building components of other systems (e.g. with commercially available building products).

POWERPACK
Compact supply module for building services to achieve technical self-sufficiency in a mobile building.

RAL
Reichs Ausschuß für Lieferbedingungen; Internationally valid quality system with color samples to aid the selection of suitable colors.

RAW CONTAINER
Unconverted version of a container.

REINFORCEMENT
Component that ensures the stability of a body under horizontally acting loads.

REMOUNTABLE
A remountable building can be reassembled again after being disassembled.

RGST
Guidelines valid in Germany relating to the process of applying for and receiving permission for the transportation of bulky and heavy loads.

SECONDARY SUPPORTING STRUCTURE
Secondary components (e.g. secondary carrier beams) that also carry loads—e.g. to provide reinforcement.

SELF-CONTAINED BUILDING SYSTEM
Building system that can only be combined with building components from its own system.

SPATIAL CELL
Building module that already has a load-bearing and surface-defining structure.

STANDARDIZATION
Adapted to generalized requirements, commonization.

STANDARD CUBE
ISO container with a standard height of 8 feet 6 inches.

STATIC LOADS
Loads caused by self-weight (e.g. self-weight of the container, of contents, weight of persons, etc.).

SYSTEM-COMPATIBLE
Complying with the regularities of the modular co-ordinations for containers.

SYSTEM OF UNITS
Uniform measurement system that provides a uniform basis for a certain purpose—e.g. the metric system (definition of the "meter" as a unit of length) or the system based on the foot.

TEMPORARY
Provisional, for a short time.

TEU
Abbreviation for Twenty-foot Equivalent Unit, an internationally standardized unit for describing the manufacturing, loading and moving capacities of freight containers; derived from the size of a 20-foot ISO container.

THERMAL SEPARATION
Reduction of the thermal flux by means of a lower heat-conducting material within a building component.

THERMAL BRIDGES
Weak points in a structure that cause increased heat losses.

TOLERANCE DIMENSION
Dimension defines the space between two assembled containers; it serves to compensate building tolerances.

TRAILER
A building site container with a chassis widely used in the USA.

TRANSPORTABLE
Transportable units have devices for transport, but do not have a chassis or similar.

TRAPEZOIDAL SHEET
Corrugated sheet manufactured from cold-rolled steel with a profile depth sufficient to provide load-bearing capacity; used as wall paneling on steel containers.

TWISTLOCK
Joining component for vertically connecting containers to each other and to the base surface in a secure, interlocking manner.

TYPE STATICS
Typical statics calculation for the load-bearing capacity of a container that is only valid for this particular model in this form; new statics calculations are necessary if modifications are carried out.

VAPOR BARRIER
Sheeting that reduces the transmission of water molecules in the form of vapor; necessary in construction to prevent the diffusion of saturated warm air from the building interior into the components of the climate shell, as otherwise vapor would condense and cause dampness in these components.

VARIABILITY
Variety of solutions in different variants.

INDEX OF PROJECTS

ADAM KALKIN
USA, www.architectureandhygiene.com

ALLFORD HALL MONAGHAN MORRIS
Great Britain, www.ahmm.co.uk

ANLSTUDIO
South Korea, www.anlstudio.com

ARCGENCY
Denmark, www.arcgency.com

ARHITEKTURA JURE KOTNIK
Slovenia, www.jurekotnik.com

ATELIER LET'S
Taiwan, atelier-lets.wixsite.com/atelier-lets/

ATELIERWORKSHOP
New Zealand, www.atelierworkshop.com

BIJVOET ARCHITECTUUR & STADSONTWERP
the Netherlands, www.wijnofwater.nl

BILLIONBRICKS
India, www.billionbricks.org/

BUREAU A
Switzerland, a-bureau.com/

BIENNALE OF INDEPENDENT SPACES FOR ART // PAGE 144
Engineer: Thomas Jundt ingénieurs civils
Client: BIG—Biennale des espaces d'art indépendants
de Genève
Completion date: 2015
Container type: shipping containers
Building volume: 1,820 m³
Number of container: 48
Construction and Material: steel containers
Photographer: courtesy of Bureau A

BUREAU DES MÉSARCHITECTURES
DIDIER FIUZA FAUSTINO
France, www.mesarchitecture.com

SKY IS THE LIMIT // PAGE 86
Completion date: 2008
Total floor area: 100 m²
Construction and materials: steel, varnished plywood,
glass, steel duckboards
Photographer: Hong Lee (05); all other photographs:
Bureau des Mésarchitectures

BWM ARCHITEKTEN
Austria, www.bwm.at/

VINOFAKTUR VOGAU // PAGE 280
BWM team: Peter Foschi, Sanja Utech, Christoph
Panzer, Gerhard Girsch, Maik Perfahl, Elena Romagnoli
Client: Vinofaktur Handel GmbH
Completion date: 2011
Photographer: Motionlab & Rupert Steiner

CASTOR DESIGN
BRIAN RICHER AND KEI NG
Canada, www.castordesign.ca

SAUNA BOX // PAGE 100
Client: many
Completion date: 2005
Total floor area: 6 m²
Building Volume: 14.5 m³
Number of containers: 1
Construction and materials: cedar, metal, glass, marble,
bronze, solar panels, wood fired stove
Construction costs: $25,000 (retail price)
Photographer: castor

CONTAINERMANUFAKTUR
Germany, www.containermanufaktur.com

CONTIKI II // PAGE 82
Architect/engineer: Containermanufaktur
Client: Mr. Weinstock
Completion date: 2019
Total floor area: 90 m²
Container type: freight 30ft bulk
Building volume: 65 m³
Number of container: 1
Structural system: PE swimmers with a steel grit
to hold the container
Construction and materials: polyethylen swimmers,
steel contstruktion, container
Building services engineering: IBW engeneering
Special features: self propelled, moveable, ready
for use throughout Europe
Photographer: Sascha Hoecker / saschahoecker.de

CONTAINERWERK EINS GMBH
Germany, containerwerk.com

RAUSCH SCHOKOLADEN COCOA ESTATE // PAGE 262
Architect: Containerwerk
Engineer: Ivan Mallinowski, Containerwerk
Client: Rausch Schokoladen GmbH
Completion Date: April 2019
Total Floor Area: approx. 104 m²
Construction Costs: €190,000
Container Type: Used sea freight containers based
on Standard Containers: 40 foot high cubes Building
Volume: approx. 460 m³
Number of Container: 4
Period of Use: long-term use
Structural System: Point foundations, sea freight
containers, steel beams
Construction and Material: Four used sea freight
containers with integrated ultra thin and monolithic
PUR high-performance insulation (patented, serial and
industrial insulation process by Containerwerk). Two
containers form the base. Two further containers lie
crosswise on the lower one.
Large glass elements are inserted in the fore fronts
of the containers, overlooking the rainforest and the
cocoa plants. The entire upper floor is surrounded by
a terrace made of regional wood.
Building Services Engineering: Containerwerk
Photographer: Gabriel Anta y Ana Santos

CUMULUS STUDIO
Australia, cumulus.studio

DEVIL'S CORNER CELLAR STUDIO // PAGE 156
Architects: Peter Walker, Liz Walsh, Andrew Geeves,
Fiona McMullen, Todd Henderson
Structural Engineering: Aldanmark
Building Surveyor: Castellan Consulting
Tourism Consultant: Simon Currant
Hospitality Consultant: David Quon
Environmental: Red Sustainability Consultants
Builder: Anstie Constructions
Client: Brown Brothers
Completion Date: 2015
Number of container: 10
Total floor area: total 572 m² (Lookout 112 m²,
Cellar Door & Market area 460 m²)
Construction and Material: repurposed and adapted
shipping containers, steel, timber
Photographer: Tanja Milbourne | Sixth Law

DEMARIA DESIGN ASSOCIATES INC.
PETER DEMARIA WITH CHRISTIAN KIENAPFEL
USA, www.demariadesign.com

REDONDO BEACH HOUSE // PAGE 264
Architect: Peter DeMaria, AIA Architekt, Dipl.-.Ing.
Christian Kienapfel, Architekt, LEED AP
Client: private client
Completion date: 2008
Total floor area: 270 m²
Number of containers: 8
Structural system: cargo container and conventional
stick frame constuction (hybrid)
Construction and materials: airplane hangar doors,
formaldehyde free plywood, recycled denim insulation/
cotton fiber insulation, multi-skinned acrylic sheets,
ceramic insulation
Construction costs: $427,000
Building services engineering: FAU
Photographer: Andre Movsesyan

GARY DEIRMENDJIAN
Australia, www.garo.com.au

CONSUMER TEMPLE – BROKEN ICON // PAGE 161
Client: invited artist, Armory Exhibition 09
Completion date: 2009
Total floor area: 12.25 m²
Building Volume: 98 m³
Photographer: Gary Deirmendjian

GRAFT ARCHITECTS
Germany, graftlab.com

BRLO BRWHOUSE // PAGE 90
Interior Design by NOVONO
Client: Braukunst Berlin Gastro GmbH
Completion date: 2017
Container type: used shipping containers
Number of Container: 38
Photographer: Seren Dal (01, 04, 05), Ulf Saupe
(02, 03, 06, 07)

GRIMME ARCHITEKTUR & MÖBELWERK-STÄTTEN
Germany, johannesgrimme.de

CONTAINERWERKSTATT // PAGE 242
Architect: Sabine and Johannes Grimme
Engineer: Dipl.-Ing. Jürgen Schröder Architekt
Client: GRIMME
Completion date: 2015
Total floor area: 336 m²
Container Type: HC High Cube Shipping Container
Building Volume: 1,382.4 m³
Number of Container: 16
Structural System: bridge fittings, no welding
between one and another container; connection points
to reinstall behind the plywood; container in the
first floor section are the static from ground floor
container
Construction and Material: fine pine plywood interior;
wood frame, super good thermal insulation floor,
wall, ceiling; statics steel;
Building Services Engineering: dustextraction for
the machine and ventilation; Bullerjan
Special Features: wood interior, mobile understructure,
full functional beauty woodshop
Photographer: Johannes Grimme

GROUP8
Switzerland, www.group8.ch

CARGO // PAGE 202
Engineer: T-IngÈnierie SA, civil engineer
Client: group8
Completion date: 2010
Total Floor Area: 783.6 m² (including containers)
Container Type: maritime containers
Building Volume: 5,390 m³ (whole office)
Photographer: Régis Golay, federal-studio.com

HAN SLAWIK / ARCHITECH
Germany, www.slawik.net

BED BY NIGHT // PAGE 188
Engineer's name: Alexander Furche
Client: State capital city of Hanover / Office
of Children's and Family Affairs
Completion date: 2001
Total floor area: 361 m²

Building Volume: 1,542 m³
Number of containers: 19
Structural system: wooden supporting structure
of laminated timber
Construction and materials: premounted industrial
glass facade
Construction costs: €192,000
Photographers: Karl Johaentges (03, 08), Han Slawik
(01, 02, 06, 09)

CAMPUS // PAGE 68
Client: Studio voor Architectuur en Techniek, Almere,
the Netherlands
Competitive price: 1986
Completion date: 1992
Number of containers: 5
Structural system: five vertically positioned 20-foot
shipping containers, combined with industrially
prefabricated building products
Photographer: Han Slawik

HOMEBOX1 // PAGE 96
Engineer's name: overall stability: Prof. A. Furche,
Köngen, Germany, Furche Zimmermann structural
engineers, Containers: Prof. E. Papsch
Completion date: 2009
Total floor area: 14.35 m²
Building Volume: 42 m³
Number of containers: 1
Structural system: wooden containers with glued
laminated timber elements with ISO corners
Construction and materials: insulation and multi-layer
panels as facade structure, wooden windows
Building services engineering: self-sufficient supply
and disposal: tanks for freshwater, rainwater and
wastewater, photovoltaic elements
Construction costs: €25,000
Photographer: Frank Aussieker/Architekturfotografie
Han Slawik (05)

HOMEBOXEN // PAGE 110
Architect/Supervisor: Han Slawik
Engineer: Ing. Douwe Dj. de Jong/Ingenicon
Completion date: 2019
Total floor area: 14.35 m² HomeBox + 5.02 m²
MicroBox = 19.37 m²
Building volume: 42.66 m³ HomeBox + 14.53 m³
MicroBox = 57.37 m³
Number of container: 2 × 20' + 2 × 8' + 1 × 6'
Structural system HomeBoxen: 20' wooden containers
with glued laminated timber elements with ISO corners
Construction and materials: insulation and multi-layer
panels as facade structure
Structural system MicroBoxen: 8' wooden frame work
with ring bolts
Building services engineering: facilities to public
supply and disposal with coupleable connections.
Heating and hot water: electric, electricity genera-
tion with photovoltaic elements on flat roofs
Construction costs: each HomeBox €35,000 + each
MicroBox €8,000 + MaterialBox €1,500 = €87,500
Photographer: architech

MYSTERY CUBE // PAGE 200
Client: Niedersächsisches Landesmuseum Hannover
Completion date: 2002
Total floor area: 52 m²
Building Volume: 295 m³
Number of containers: 4
Structural system: stacked building containers
Construction and materials: standard construction
scaffolding surrounded by integrated stairs, covered
with a black fiber-glass fabric
Construction costs: €15,700 + €390 for equipment

HAN SLAWIK
With IMS Ingenieurgesellschaft mbh
and BOF Architekten

IBA DOCK // PAGE 252
Realisation: bof architekten, Bücking Ostrop Flemming
Engineer's name: IMS Ingenieurgesellschaft mbH
Client: IBA Hamburg GmbH, Internationale
Bauausstellung
Completion date: 2010
Total floor area: 1,831 m²
Building Volume: 6,855 m³
Number of containers: 36 × 60 foot containerframes
Structural system: modular construction with steel
frames
Construction costs: €8 million
Photography: KLEUSBERG GmbH & Co. KG – photographer
Rüdiger Mosler (03, 04, 05)

HELEN & HARD ARCHITEKTEN
Norway, www.hha.no

B-CAMP // PAGE 182
Engineer's name: Dimensjon Rådgivning
Client: Helen & Hard ANS
Completion date: 2004
Total floor area: 140 m²
Building Volume: 380 m³
Number of containers: 8
Structural system: structural containers stacked
on top of each other
Construction and materials: dwelling containers from
offshore industry, fitted with second hand windows and
doors. cladding: transparent corrugated plastic panels,
and scrap metal from metal industry.
Construction costs: €200,000
Photographer: Emile Ashley

HOLZER KOBLER ARCHITEKTUREN
ZÜRICH/BERLIN
Switzerland/Germany, holzerkobler.com

DESIGN HOSTEL // PAGE 104
Interior Design and Color concept: Kinzo Architekten
GmbH, Berlin
Client: Immobilienverwaltung Köster & Nissen GbR
Completion date: 2017
Total floor area: 4,316 m²
Container type: 40' × 8' × 9'6" ISO Type Dry Cargo Steel
Container
Building volume: 13,240 m³
Number of container: 76 (61 rooms: 37 double rooms,
18 four-bed-dorms, 4 eight-bed-dorms, 2 suites)
Structural system: recycled containers in a steel-
concrete-structure
Construction and materials: steel, concrete
Site Agent: PMR Projektmanagement Rostock GmbH,
Rostock
Structural Design: Ingenieurbüro Hippe, Berlin
Building Technology: Ingenieurbüro Hartmann, Rostock
Electronical Engineering: Ingenieurgesellschaft
Hartmann mbH, Berlin
Fire Protection: Rössel Brandschutz, Berlin
Building Physics: Müller-BBM GmbH, Berlin
Structural Design, Steel Construction: Ingenieurbüro
für Statik, Konstruktion und Bauphysik Dipl.-Ing.
Andreas Leipold, Berlin
Steel structure: HAB Wusterhusen, Wusterhusen
Dry wall installation: Knauf Gips KG, Iphofen
Window construction: Metallbau Rostock GmbH, Rostock
Concrete components: fdu GmbH & Co. KG,
Georgsmarienhütte
Elevator: Schindler Aufzüge und Fahrtreppen GmbH,
Hamburg

Facade: Schüco International KG, Weißenfels
Ventilation engineer: Wilfried Hubert Ingenieurbüro
für Gebäude- und Umwelttechnik, Bentwisch
PHOTOGRAPHER: Jan Bitter

I IN INC
Japan, i-in.jp

SCHMATZ TOKYO DOME // PAGE 54
Engineer: AICS.inc
Client: Kaiser Kitchen K.K.
Completion date: 2018
Total Floor Area: 28 m²
Container Type: freight container
Number of Container: 2
Photographer: Tomooki Kengak

IMS INGENIEURGESELLSCHAFT MBH
AND BOF ARCHITEKTEN
Germany, www.bof-architekten.de

RESEARCH STATION // PAGE 260
Engineer's name: m+p consulting, Braunschweig
Client: NCAOR/National Centre for Antarctic & Ocean
Research, Goa, India
Completion date: 2011/2012
Total floor area: 2,150 m²
Building Volume: Including outer shell: 7,850 m³
Number of containers: 132 containers (20 feet),
the corridors in the upper stories consist of "flats"
Structural system: containers are used to provide
the supporting structure. The protruding part of the
station has an additional steel supporting structure
with V supports.
Building services engineering: the building has three
combined heat and power units for back-up purposes
that generate the electricity required. The waste
heat from the CHP units is harnessed and used to heat
the station. In addition, the station is fitted with
ventilation equipment, and the air-conditioning main-
tains an air humidity of around 30%. Drinking water
is produced from seawater using a desalination unit,
and waste water treatment is also carried out.

JAMES & MAU ARCHITECTS
Chile, www.jamesandmau.com

INFINISKI MANIFESTO HOUSE // PAGE 106
Client: private
Completion date: 2009
Total floor area: 160 m²
Construction costs: €550/m² in Chile.
€750/m² in Europe
Photographer: Antonio Corcuera

JON DARSKY
USA, www.delpopolosf.com

DEL POPOLO // PAGE 56
Engineer: Mclellan Industries
COMPLETION DATE: 2012
NUMBER OF CONTAINER: 1
CONSTRUCTION AND MATERIAL: metal and glass
Photographer: courtesy of Jon Darsky

KNOCK
Sweden, www.knock.se

VOLVO C30 EXPERIENCE PAVILION // PAGE 212
Engineer's name: Space Display
Client: Volvo Cars, www.volvocars.com
Completion date: 2006
Total floor area: 468m²
Number of containers: 54 and a 50m long hallway
where the guests entered the event
Photographer: KNOCK, Mikael Olsson

LHVH ARCHITEKTEN
Germany, www.lhvh.de

DERCUBE // PAGE 201
Client: derCube AG/KulturFlecken Silberstern e.V.,
Freudenberg
Completion date: 2007
Total floor area: 400m²
Building Volume: 1,500m³
Number of containers: 36
Structural system: steel frame structure (30 contain-
ers, 6 stair towers, ALHO Systembau-Basic line)
Construction and materials: standard construction dry
mortarless construction, HPL boardan walls and ceilings,
PVC floors, EPS pressure cloth front
Building services engineering: Standard power and
water supply, structural sunscreen by pressure
cloth front
Construction costs: €495,000
Photographer: Axel Ollenschläger

SEVEN-DAY ARCHITECTURE // PAGE 206
Client: ALHO Systembau, Friesenhagen
Completion date: 2004
Total floor area: 725m²
Building Volume: 2,610m³
Number of containers: 48
Structural system: steel-frame supporting structure (29
construction site office containers, 17 frames, 3 stair-
well towers, ALHO Systembau-Basic line)
Construction and materials: 1st floor and 2nd floor:
Standard drywall construction, high-pressure laminate
sheets on the walls and ceilings, PVC floor; 3rd floor:
finishing in accordance with the German energy saving
ordinance standard, drywall construction with corre-
sponding insulation on the ceilings and walls, linoleum
floor, full-length window, cloth facade
Building services engineering: standard electricity and
water supply, in-built sun protection from cloth facade
Construction costs: €495,000
Photographer: ALHO Systembau/Mr. Schade

LOT-EK
USA, www.lot-ek.com

CARROLL HOUSE // PAGE 74
Design: LOT-EK, Ada Tolla + Giuseppe Lignano, Principals,
Virginie Stolz, Project Architect
Commission: Kim and Joe Carroll
Size: 5,000 SF indoor + 2,500 SF outdoor
Structural Engineer: SILMAN
MEP/Sustainability: Dagher
Completion: 2017
Number of container: 21
Photographer: Danny Bright

DRIVELINES STUDIOS // PAGE 222
Design: LOT-EK, Ada Tolla + Giuseppe Lignano, Principals,
Sara Valente, Project Architect
Commission: PROPERTUITY
Size: 75,000 sqft
Completion: 2017

Consultants: Structural Engineer: Asakheni + Silman
MEP: VBK Engineering Systems + ABBINK Consulting
Project Management: SevenBar Consulting
Architect of record: Anita du Plessis
Fire: Drofnets Engineering
Civil: DG Consulting Engineers
Construction: Tri-Star
Photographer: Dave Southwood

MDU/MOBILE DWELLING UNIT // PAGE 79
Engineer's name: engineering + fabrication: UAF Con-
struction/Marc Ganzglass
Completion date: 2003
Total floor area: 46m²
Structural system: modified shipping container
Construction and materials: shipping container,
plywood, nudo boards, fluorescent lights
Construction costs: $150,000
Number of containers: 1
Photographer: courtesy of the Walker Art Center

PUMA CITY // PAGE 162
Engineer's name: structure: Robert Silman Associates,
MEP: David Rosini
Client: PUMA
Completion date: 2008
Total floor area: 1,020m²
Number of containers: 24
Structural system: reinforced shipping containers
Construction and materials: shipping containers,
apitong wood, galvanized steel stairs, LED lights
Photographer: Danny Bright

QIYUN MOUNTAIN CAMP // PAGE 138
Design: LOT-EK, Ada Tolla + Giuseppe Lignano, Principals,
Virginie Stolz, Project Architect
Commission: ZYJ Sunriver
Size: 75,000 SF, with 5,000 SF Entrance Pavilion,
35,000 SF Market, 15,000 SF Restaurant, 5,000 SF
Aquatic Pier
Completion: 2017
Consultants: Structural
Engineering: Robert Silman Associates
Fabrication: ArchiSpace
Photography: Noah Sheldon

SANLITUN SOUTH // PAGE 254
Engineer's name: Beijing Architectural & Engineering
Design Company
Client: Guo Feng
Completion date: 2008
Total floor area: 24,000m²
Number of containers: 151
Structural system: reinforced concrete structure with
modified shipping containers
Photographer: Shuhe Architectural Photography

UNIQLO FLAGSHIP // PAGE 60
Engineer's name: Shimizu Building Life Care Kansai
Client: UNIQLO
Completion date: 2004
Total floor area: 1,022m²
Number of containers: 1

UNIQLO POP-UP STORES // PAGE 60
Engineer's name: engineering + fabrication:
TRS Containers
Client: UNIQLO
Completion date: 2006
Total floor area: 30m²
Number of containers: 1 per unit
Structural system: modified shipping container
Construction and materials: shipping container, plywood,
nudo board shelves, fluorescent lights, retractable
duct dressing room
Construction costs: €29,000
Photographer: Danny Bright

LUC DELEU
Belgium, www.topoffice.to

CONSTRUCTION X // PAGE 160
Engineer's name: Dirk Jaspaert
Client: Middelheim open air sculpture museum,
Antwerp, Belgium
Completion date: 2003
Number of containers: 9
Construction and materials: containers, twistlocks,
screw bridge fittings, stacking cones, special inter-
connecting devices
Photographer: Philippe de Gobert

HOORN BRIDGE // PAGE 160
Engineer's name: Dirk Jaspaert
Client: organization of the exhibition "For real now"
Completion date: 1990
Total floor area: 30m²
Number of containers: 2
Construction and materials: containers (back wall
removed), screw bridge fittings, special inter-
connecting devices
Photographer: Wim Riemens

ORBINO // PAGE 142
Engineer's name: Dirk Jaspaert
Completion date: 2004
Total floor area: 45m²
Construction and materials: containers (three remodeled
containers), screw bridge fittings, stacking cones,
steel staircase, concrete base
Photographer: Han Slawik

SPEYBANK // PAGE 160
Engineer's name: Dirk Jaspaert
Client: open air sculpture, Museum Middelheim, Antwerp,
Belgium
Completion: 2003
Number of containers: 4 × 20-foot containers
Construction and materials: containers, screw bridge
fittings, stacking cones, concrete base, special
interconnecting devices.
Photographer: Philippe de Gobert

LUIS RODRÍGUEZ ALONSO, JAVIER PRESA
Spain

KIOWA PROTOTYPE (HABITAINER) // PAGE 78
Completion date: 2006
Total floor area: 14m²
Building Volume: 30m³
Number of containers: 1
Structural system: container structural chasis,
selfstanding dinamic groundation feet
Construction and materials: steel 20-foot container
1BB. Internal panel system composite on polyurethane,
polystyrene, wood frame and Medium Density recycled
fiber board. White matte paint finish on ceiling and
walls. Plastic continuous floor finish. Electric-
ity protection board + 3 lines interior conductions.
WC, toilet and shower units. Steel plumbing exterior
conduction.
Construction costs: €8,000
Photographer: Pablo Rodríguez

MARIA JOSE TREJOS ARCHITECT
Costa Rica, www.mariajosetrejos.com

INCUBO HOUSE // PAGE 178
Engineer: Shalini Tahilramani
Client: Professional Photographer
Completion Date: 2012
Total Floor Area : 340m²

Container Type: 40ft containers
Number Of Container: 8
Structural System: concrete foundations, steel frames, containers
Construction And Material: steel and concrete
Special Features: solar heat water, rain water collection, cross ventilation, refraction roof, plastic and wood recycled decking, led lightning, bamboo floors for bedrooms, concrete floor for social areas, foam and aluminum system for interior isolation
Photographer: courtesy of Maria Jose Trejos Architect

MARMOL RADZINER PREFAB
USA, www.marmol-radziner.com,
www.marmolradzinerfurniture.com

HIDDEN VALLEY // PAGE 240
Client: private
Completion date: 2007
Total floor area: indoor 230m², terraces 160m²
Number of containers: 15 moduls
Structural system: recycled-steel frame modules, made in a factory, shipped complete
Construction and materials: main house: 12 recycled steel-framed modules, garage: 3 modules, metal panel siding, ipe wood decks, sadlestone floors, walnut casework, caesarstone countertops, geothermal ground loop HVAC and pool heating system, kw solar planel array backup generator, 900 feet well and 1700 gallon cistern
Building services engineering: general contractor: Marmol Radziner, mechanical engineer: Trey Austin, electrical engineer: Nikolakopulos, structural engineer: C.W.Howe
Photographer: Joe Fletcher

MEYER EN VAN SCHOOTEN ARCHITECTEN
The Netherlands, mvsa-architects.com

TEMPORARY ACCOMMODATION FOR 1001 DAYS // PAGE 210
Client: Meyer en Van Schooten Architecten, Amsterdam
Completion date: 2000
Total floor area: 800m²
Building Volume: 5,000m³
Number of containers: 10 containers + 1 as entrance
Structural system: the formar factory hall was used as the outer skin/space for the project. The structure of the 10 sea containers was used to construct the spaces within the space.
Contractor, builder: Bouwbedrijf E.A. van den Hengel bv, Soest
Construction costs: €154,800 +/- €195 per m²
Photographers: Luuk Kramer (03, 04, 05);© Hans Fonk (02, 06)
Drawings: Meyer en van Schooten Architecten

MM+P / MEYER-MIETHKE & PARTNER
Germany

50,000 € MODULAR-HOUSE // PAGE 207
Completion date: 2000-2002

MOUAZ ABOUZAID, BASSEL OMARA, AHMED HAMMAD
Dubai/United Arab Emirates, www.sheltainer.com

SHELTAINERS // PAGE 282
Gross built area: 500,000 m²
Awards: 2nd Prize Future Hose Micro House 2017; Winner - WAFx Ethics & Value Category 2018; Shortlisted in WAF 18 world architecture festival "Competition Entry Category"; Highly Commended Middle East Architect Award Concept design & Sustainable project of the year 2017-2018; Honourable mention Cairo Design Award 2018

MVRDV
the Netherlands, www.mvrdv.nl

CANCER CENTER AMSTERDAM // PAGE 198
Engineer's name: De Meeuw
Client: Cancer Center Amsterdam, the Netherlands
Completion date: 2005
Total floor area: 6,000m²
Number of containers: 256
Photographer: Rob 't Hart

NICHOLAS LACEY AND PARTNERS
Great Britain, www.containercity.com

TRINITY BUOY WHARF (CONTAINER CITY I) // PAGE 190
Engineer's name: Buro Happold
Client: Urban Space Management Ltd.
Completion date: 2001
Total floor area: 450m²
Number of containers: 20
Photographer: Teresa Lundquist

TRINITY BUOY WHARF (CONTAINER CITY II) // PAGE 190
Engineer's name: Buro Happold
Client: Urban Space Management Ltd.
Completion date: 2002
Number of containers: 30
Photographer: Teresa Lundquist

NORTH ARROW STUDIO
USA, northarrowstudio.com

CONTAINER BAR // PAGE 250
Design: Hendley/Knowles Design Studio
Completion date: 2014
Photographer: courtesy of North Arrow Studio

PATZNER ARCHITEKTEN
Germany, www.patzner-architekten.de

BORNACK DROP STOP TRAINING CENTER // PAGE 80
Engineer's name: Wulle Ingenieure
Client: Bornack GmbH+Co. KG
Completion date: 2006
Total floor area: entire building approx. 6,500m²
Containers approx. 150m²
Building Volume: Entire building 110,000m³, containers 375m³
Number of containers: 10
Construction costs: ca. €300,000 (conversion costs)
Photographer: Stefan Hohloch

PAUL STANKEY, SARAH NORDBY
USA, www.innateworks.com

HOLYOKE CABIN // PAGE 98
Engineer's name: Scott Stankey, Krista Stankey
Client: Paul Stankey, Scott Stankey, Krista Stankey, Sarah Nordby
Completion date: 2000
Number of containers: 2
Structural system: steel and wood
Construction and materials: concrete, steel, wood, glass
Construction costs: $20,000

PEOPLE'S ARCHITECTURE OFFICE
China, www.peoples-architecture.com

CONTAINER STACK PAVILION // PAGE 256
Architect: He Zhe, James Shen, Zang Feng
Client: Eastern Heights Real Estate Co. Ltd.
Completion Date: 2015
Total Floor Area: 307.3 m²
Photographer: People's architecture office

PHOOEY ARCHITECTS
Australia, www.phooey.com.au

CHILDREN'S ACTIVITY CENTRE // PAGE 118
Engineer's name: Perrett Simpson Consulting Engineers
Client: City of Port Phillip
Completion date: 2007
Total floor area: 127m²
Number of containers: 4
Structural system: re-used freight container
Construction and materials: material durable, recycled, reclaimed, plantation, reused or salvaged from demolition; this included decking, windows, carpet tiles and joinery. The whole container was re-used including doors suspending balconies. As a process of feedback design, the container off-cuts (with cannibalised super scale graphics) were recycled into the final building. Container off-cuts were re-fashioned into functional balustrades, sun shading and decoration. Timber deck off-cuts became soffit linings.
Construction costs: €83,000
Photographer: Peter Bennetts

PIERRE MORENCY ARCHITECTE
Canada, pierremorencyarchitecte.com

CHALET DU CHEMIN BROCHU // PAGE 268
Client: Pierre Morency
Completion date: 2007
Total floor area: 160m²
Number of containers: 3
Structural system: foundation and piloti
Construction and materials: concrete foundation, container, hemlock as a second skin, steel columns to hold the third container
Construction costs: €85,000
Photographer: Normand Rajotte

PLATOON.BERLIN & SOEREN ROEHRS
Germany, www.platoon.org

PLATOON CULTURAL DEVELOPMENT BERLIN // PAGE 122
Client: PLATOON
Completion date: first status 2002, last 2007
Total floor area: 110m²
Building Volume: 280m³
Number of containers: 4 + 1 pool

Structural system: no additional enforcement
Construction and materials: wooden frame work,
plywood, filled with cellulose, planked with
aluminum cover
Construction costs: €80,000
Building services engineering: aircondition
heating system
Photographer: Christian v. Steffelin

PLATOON AND GRAFT ARCHITECTS
WITH U-IL ARCHITECTS
Germany, www.platoon.org

PLATOON KUNSTHALLE SEOUL // PAGE 148
Architect: PLATOON in collaboration with GRAFT Archi-
tects, Beijing + U-il Architects, Seoul, South Korea
Engineer's name: Midas IT, Seoul, South Korea
Client: PLATOON cultural development
Completion date: 2009
Total floor area: 950m²
Building Volume: 3,600m³
Number of containers: 28
Structural system: reinforced cargo containers
stacked and welded
Construction and materials: frame work, plasterboard,
mineral wool, covered with aluminium plates
Building services engineering: main hall floor heating,
cooling ventilation by open garage doors; container
rooms with cooling & warming air condition; complete
sanitary installations + restaurant kitchen
Construction costs: €715,000
Photographer: PLATOON

PLUS+ BAUPLANUNG
WITH ENGELHARDT.EGGLER.ARCHITEKTEN.
Germany, www.plus-bauplanung.de

THEATERHAUS STUTTGART // PAGE 84
Engineer's name: supporting structure: Löffler
Ingenieur Consult GmbH, existing supporting
Structure: Dr.Ing. Adrian Pocanschi
Client: Stiftung Pragsattel Theaterhaus
Completion date: 2003
Total floor area: 12,200m²
Building Volume: standard freight container
Number of containers: 1
Construction costs: net construction and associated
costs, theater building with "Musik der Jahrhunderte"
approx. €15 million, administration with restaurant
approx. €2 million
Building services engineering: air-conditioning and
ventilation concept
Photographer: Dietmar Strauss / Bildermacher
Architekturfotografie

PLAYZE
Germany, www.playze.com

TONY'S FARM // PAGE 278
Team: Mengjia He, Pascal Berger, Marc Schmit, Meijun Wu,
Liv Xu Ye, Ahmed Hosny, Andres Tovar, Maggie Tang,
Sebastian Hefti
Client: Tony's Farm
Completion date: 2011
Built area: 1,060m²
Number of container: 78
Photographer: Bartosz Kolonko

RAUMLABORBERLIN
JAN LIESEGANG AND MATTHIAS RICK
Germany, www.raumlabor.net

EICHBAUMOPER // PAGE 154
Engineer's names: implementation planning: Jan
Liesegang, Matthias Rick (both of raumlaborberlin),
Jan Stauf (Gesellschaft der Holzfreunde), Christian
Rick (Raantec), construction statics: Necati Elitas
Client: "Eichbaumoper" production company
Completion date: 2008
Total floor area: 50m²
Building Volume: 160m³
Number of containers: 4
Structural system: Container frame system with partial
steel-structure reinforcements
Construction and materials: Interior insulation,
wooden battens, insulating material, vapor barrier,
drywall, simple planking
Building services technology: electrical, mobile
counter/bar with water tank
Construction costs: €70,000
Photographer: Matthias Rick

RENNER HAINKE WIRTH ARCHITEKTEN
Germany, www.rhwarchitekten.de

CRUISE CENTER // PAGE 230
Engineer's name: supporting structure: Werner
Sobek Ingenieure, Stuttgart, fire protection: HPP,
Braunschweig, building services technology:
HHLA, Hamburg
Client: Hafencity Hamburg GmbH
Completion date: 2004
Total floor area: 1,500m²
Building Volume: 15,300m³
Number of containers: 48
Structural system: supporting structure made of
20-foot and 40-foot freight containers; used
containers stacked to form three layers; loaded with
ballast to counteract wind and lever forces; extended
using retrofitted steel frames in container dimen-
sions; roof-supporting structure with wooden truss
design, mounted on perimeter steel support.
Construction and materials: building with no climate
shell; existing asphalt ground with bright red
polyurethane coating; carpet in container, container
with maritime blue-to-green tones on the outside;
roof covering with steel sandwich covering and
translucent twin-wall sheets.
Construction costs: €1.2 million + €0.6 million for site
Building services engineering: Indoors not heated
Photographer: Fotodesign Christoph Gebler

RIVER & RAIN
Bangladesh, riverandrain.net

ESCAPE DEN // PAGE 274
Architect: Kazi Fida Islam
Engineer: Eng. Shah Alam, Eng. Ruhul Alam
Client: Mr. Tanjim Ashraful Haque & Ms. Asma Sultana
Completion Date: 2017
Total Floor Area: 317.84 sq m
Container Type: 40' × 9.5', 20' × 9.5' freight containers
Number of Container: 4
Structural System: steel frame skeletons
Construction and Material: locally manufactured
materials, shipping containers from depots, engineered
wood, abandoned shipping decks
Photographer: Maruf Raihan, Hasan Saifudding Chandan,
Sayed Asif Mahmud

ROBERT DUKE ARCHITECT
WITH KIETH DOYLE, IAIN SINCLAIR, NICOLE MION AND
EVANN SIEBENS
Canada, www.containr.com
CONTAINR CINEMA // PAGE 136
Creative Team: Robert Duke Architect, Kieth Doyle,
Iain Sinclair
Artistic Director/Curator: Nicole Mion, Evann Siebens
Engineer's name: Bush, Bohlman & Partners Consulting
Structural Engineers
Client: presented by Springboard in partnership with
the Vancouver 2009 Cultural Olympiad
Completion date: 2009
Number of containers: 2

ROSS STEVENS
New Zealand

CONTAINER HOUSE (KILLER HOUSE) // PAGE 124
Engineer's name: Rob Bryant, TSE Group
Client: Ross Stevens
Completion date: 2006
Total floor area: 90m² insulated, 45m² covered
verandah, 60m² garage
Number of containers: 3 containers + 3 shipping
platforms
Structural system: 3 vertically stacked containers
elevated 3m off ground level on re-used industrial
crane sections
Construction and materials: re-used steel,
aluminium and polycarbonate
Construction costs: NZ$200,000
Photographer: Petra Alsbach-Stevens

SCULP(IT) ARCHITECTEN
Belgium, www.sculp.it

LIVE/WORK SPACE // PAGE 134
Engineer's name: Stubeco bvba
Client: Peerlings-Mertens
Completion date: 2007
Total floor area: 60m²
Building Volume: 180m³
Structural system: steelstructure
Construction and materials: wooden beams, wooden floors
(parket), brick walls (existing), concrete floor
Construction costs: €125,000
Photographer: Luc Roymans

SEAN GODSELL
Australia, www.seangodsell.com

FUTURE SHACK // PAGE 102
Completion date: 2001
Total floor area: 15m²
Structural system: steel
Photographer: Earl Carter

SEBASTIAN IRARRAZAVAL
Chile, www.sebastianirarrazaval.net

CASA ORUGA // PAGE 112
Architect: Sebastián Irarrázaval Delpiano
Associated Architect: Erick Caro.
Client: Ricardo Bezanilla
Structural Engineer: Pedro Bartolomé
Construction: Sebastián Irarrázaval Arquitectos
Site Supervision: Ricardo Carril
Materials: 5 × 40 "standard shiping containers, 6 × 20
"standard shiping containers and 1 × 40" open top

shiping container , steel plates , concrete retaining
walls, and gypsum board , tymber wood
Site area: 900m²
Gross Built area: 350m²
Completion date: 2012
Photographer: Sergio Pirrone

SERDA ARCHITECTS
Austria, www.serda.at

SPACEMAN SPIFF // PAGE 94
Completion date: 1997
Photographer: Architect Alexander Eduard Serda

SHE-ARCHITEKTEN
ULRICH HAHNEFELD, MARCO PAWLIK, STEPHEN PERRY,
STEPHAN SCHRICK AND TORSTEN STERN
Germany, www.she-architekten.com

ARCHITEKTURBOX // PAGE 186
Engineer's name: WTM Engineers GmbH
Client: Initiative Hamburger Architektur Sommer e.V.
Completion date: 2006
Total floor area: 85m²
Building Volume: 250m³
Number of containers: 5
Structural system: system structure
Construction and materials: material collage
Photographer: Oliver Heissner

SHIGERU BAN ARCHITECTS
Japan, www.shigerubanarchitects.com

NOMADIC MUSEUM // PAGE 218
Architect: Shigeru Ban Architects
Engineer's name: Buro Happold
Completion date: 2005
Total floor area: 3,020m²
Structural system: steel container (wall)
Construction and materials: PVC membrane (roof, wall)
plywood (wall), paper tube, water seal coated (columns)
gravel, wood plank deck (floor)
Photographer: Michael Moran Photography, inc.

SHIGERU BAN ARCHITECTS +
KACI INTERNATIONAL INC.
Japan, www.shigerubanarchitects.com

PAPERTAINER MUSEUM // PAGE 226
Architect: Shigeru Ban Architects +
KACI International Inc.
Engineer's name: Minoru Tezuka, Myung-Hwan Lee
(SAMHYUN TG)
Client: Design House Inc.
Sponsor: Seoul Metropolitan City, SOSFO, SAMSUNG
Electronics
Completion date: 2006
Total floor area: 3,820m²
Structural system: foundation-steel beam frame
10 in container box + 40 in container box for roof
paper tube column and paper tube roof truss
Photographer: Design House Inc.

SPILLMANN ECHSLE ARCHITEKTEN
Switzerland, www.spillmannechsle.ch

FREITAG FLAGSHIP STORE ZURICH // PAGE 128
Engineer's name: Henauer Gugler Zürich
Client: Freitag lab AG
Completion date: 2006
Total floor area: 120m²
Number of containers: 17
Construction costs: €400,000
Photographer: Roland Tännler

STUDIO EDWARDS
Australia, www.studio-edwards.com

HOUSE 28 // PAGE 272
Number of container: 3
Container type: 20 ft shipping container
Photographer: Tony Gorsevski

TEMPOHOUSING / JMW ARCHITEKTEN
the Netherlands, www.tempohousing.com

KEETWONEN // PAGE 194
Engineer's name: Tempohousing
Client: Housing association De Key in Amsterdam
Completion date: 2006
Total floor area: 31,000m²
Building Volume: 80,600m³
Number of containers: 1,030
Structural system: self containing, no super structure
necessary; steel shell (containers) have a special
Tempohousing design (front and rear frame reinforced)
Construction and materials: stacked containers, steel-
frame balconies and walkways and staircases, foundation
on prefab concrete piles; additional steelframe roof
trusses with insulated panels
Construction costs: €20.8 million ex VAT
Building services engineering: per 150 container
homes, 1 container with heating boilers (natural gas
fuelled) that feed all the individual containers.
Temperature per container to be adjusted. Each
container individual mechanical ventilation with
automatic variable speeds. Each container a 4 group
fuse box. Hot water per container with electric
heated tank of 50 liters. Cooking on electrical
stove. All units have their own bathroom (shower,
toilet, sink) and their own kitchen.
Photographer: Tempohousing

TRS STUDIO
Peru, www.behance.net/trsworkshop

PACHACUTEC HOUSE // PAGE 50
Photographer: All images are 3D RENDERS BY BINEURAL 3D

URBANTAINER AND OFFICE 53427
South Korea, www.urbantainer.com,
www.office-53427.com/

COMMON GROUND // PAGE 166
Space design: Younjjin Jeong, Bohyung Kim, Soyeon Song,
Eunhye Choi
Brand design: Younjjin Jeong, Yang Didi, Minjeong Choi,
Yejee Lee
Landscape: Live Space
Completion date: 2016
Photographer: Kyungsub Shin

WHITAKER STUDIO
Great Britain, www.whitakerstudio.co.uk

JOSHUA TREE RESIDENCE // PAGE 130
Engineer: Concept engineering advice by Arup
Client: Private Client
Completion date: 2020 (estimated)
Total Floor Area: 200m²
Construction Costs: Estimated $1,000,000
Container Type: 40ft high top freight containers
Building Volume: 450m³
Number of Container: 19
Structural System: Precut and then site welded
Construction and Material: Plasterboard and polished
concrete floor

WOLFGANG LATZEL ARCHITEKTEN
WOLFGANG LATZEL, NORBERT ZSCHORNACK
Germany, www.latzelarchitekten.de

FLYPORT // PAGE 234
Engineer's name: Bearing structure: Herbert Fink,
Berlin; Building equipment and appliances:
Büro Kleemann, Berlin
Completion date: Planing since 2004
Total floor area: 4,200m² (prototype)
Building Volume: 25,000m³ (prototype)
Number of containers: 410 (prototype)
Structural system: Steel frame construction consisting
of moduls
Construction and materials: Standardized passenger
terminal; three standards have been developed: high,
medium and basic standard, depending on the demands
of the user or operator.
Building services engineering: Standard equipment
in heating, air conditioning, sanitation, electric,
additional airport specific systems
Construction costs: starting from 2,000€/m²
(incl. planing, add. transportation)

EDITORS

Prof. Han Slawik

Diploma in Architecture at the Technical University of Braunschweig/D 1973. Architect in several offices. Scientific assistant at the Technical University of Dortmund. 1984–1994 Professor at Coburg University/D. 1994–2009 Professor of Design and Construction at Leibniz University in Hanover/D. 1986 first "Campus" steel container house in Almere/NL. Pioneer project of container architecture. Studio for Architecture and Technology–*architech*–in Bad Bentheim/D. and Amsterdam/NL. Experimental buildings and projects. Numerous international publications, awards, prizes, lectures on container architecture and modular construction. Participation in the Architecture Biennale Venice with container buildings in 2004, in the Architecture Biennial Sao Paulo 2011, in the Architecture Exhibition "Living Spaces Today" in Havana/Cuba 2016, in the Traveling Exhibition in Cuba 2017 and in the BouwEXPO Tiny Housing in Almere 2019. Pioneer of container architecture.

Dipl.-Ing. Julia Bergmann

Born 1971. Degree in architecture from the Technical University Braunschweig/D 1999. Work for different architecture offices. 2003 establishment of an office in Berlin/D. Reasonably priced single-family homes made of steel in cooperation with the office kleyer.koblitz.architekten. Various awards and recognitions. 2004–2009 Research Associate with Prof. Slawik, Institute for Design and Construction, Department of Experimental Design and Engineering and 2009–2015 with Prof. Schumacher, Department of Civil Engineering. Teaching assignment at Leibniz University Hanover/D. Since 2015 he has been working for schneider + schumacher in Frankfurt/D., focusing on low-cost residential construction with a research share. Realization of cost-effective new residential construction, re-usage, and urban redevelopment.

Dipl.-Ing. Matthias Buchmeier

Born 1977. Degree in architecture from the Leibniz University Hanover/D 2005. Since 2005 freelance work as an architect for different architecture offices. Freelance cooperation with various architectural firms. Collaboration on various container projects in the office *architech* Prof. Han Slawik. 2008–2009 Research Associate with Prof. Slawik, Leibniz University Hanover/D., Institute for Design and Construction, Department of Experimental Design and Engineering. Since 2013 guest lecturer Architecture and Resources, Alanus College of Art & Society, Alfter near Bonn/D.

Dipl.-Ing. Sonja Tinney

Born 1974. Studied abroad in 2004/2005 at the Universitá IUAV di Venezia/Italy. Degree in architecture from Leibniz University Hanover 2006. Freelance work for different architecture offices. Since 2006 collaboration in diverse container construction projects at the office of Prof. Han Slawik. Since 2008 scientific assistant to Prof. Slawik at the Institute of Design and Construction, Experimental Design and Construction Section at Leibniz University Hanover/D.

CONTAINER ATLAS
A PRACTICAL GUIDE TO CONTAINER ARCHITECTURE

This book was conceived, edited, and designed by gestalten.

Edited by Han Slawik, Julia Bergmann, Matthias Buchmeier,
Sonja Tinney, and by Lukas Feireiss and Robert Klanten for gestalten

Texts by Han Slawik, Julia Bergmann, Matthias Buchmeier,
and Sonja Tinney
Project descriptions by Shonquis Moreno and
Eliora Stuhler for gestalten
The History of the Shipping Container by Kitty Bolhöfer for gestalten
Guest contribution *Structural Engineering and Freight Containers*
by Douwe de Jong

Translation from German to English by Patrick Sheehan and
Alexandra Walter
Editorial Management by Julian Sorge and
Lars Pietzschmann for gestalten
Design by Birga Meyer for gestalten
Layout by Natalie Reed and Melanie Ullrich for gestalten
Typefaces: Bonesana by Matthieu Cortat, T-Star Mono Round
by Mika Mischler, Generika Mono by Alexander Meyer

Cover motif: Joshua Tree Residence by Whitaker Studio
Backcover images from top left to bottom right by Maria Jose Trejos Architect,
TRS Studio (Bineural 3D), Bureau des Mésarchitectures, People's Architecture
Office, River & Rain, Jon Darsky

Printed by Gutenberg Beuys Feindruckerei GmbH, Langenhagen
Made in Germany

Published by gestalten, Berlin 2020
ISBN 978-3-89955-669-8
Updated edition

For more information, and to order books, please visit www.gestalten.com

Bibliographic information published by the Deutsche Nationalbibliothek.
The Deutsche Nationalbibliothek lists this publication in the Deutsche National-
bibliografie; detailed bibliographic data is available online at www.dnb.de

None of the content in this book was published in exchange for payment by
commercial parties or designers; gestalten selected all included work based
solely on its artistic merit.

This book was printed on paper certified according to the standards of the FSC®.